GREATER THINGS THAN THESE

By the same author

BOOKS

THE LITURGY OF PENANCE, Faith Press, 1966.
THE FEAST OF PENTECOST, Faith Press, 1967.
CHRISTMAS AND EPIPHANY, Faith Press, 1967.
COMMENTARY ON THE NEW LECTIONARY, S.P.C.K.,
     Volume 1, 1973; Volume 2, 1974.

CONTRIBUTIONS

'Charisms and Confirmation' in CRISIS FOR CONFIRMA-
     TION, ed. Michael Perry, S.C.M. Press, 1967.

'Catholics in the Church of England' in CATHOLIC
     ANGLICANS TODAY, ed. John Wilkinson, Darton,
     Longman & Todd, 1968.

'The Changing Liturgy of Penance' in PENANCE: VIRTUE
     AND SACRAMENT, ed. John Fitzsimons, Burns &
     Oates, 1969.

'The Penitential Rite' in SERIES THREE ESSAYS, ed.
     Ronald Jasper, S.P.C.K., 1974.

GREATER THINGS THAN THESE

A PERSONAL ACCOUNT OF THE CHARISMATIC MOVEMENT

BY

JOHN GUNSTONE

FOREWORD BY
THE ARCHBISHOP OF CANTERBURY

THE FAITH PRESS
Leighton Buzzard, Beds LU7 7NQ
MOREHOUSE-BARLOW CO. INC., NEW YORK, U.S.A.

First published in 1974
© *John Gunstone, 1974*

PRINTED IN GREAT BRITAIN
in 10pt. Times type
BY THE FAITH PRESS LTD.
LEIGHTON BUZZARD LU7 7NQ

SBN 7164 0285 8

CONTENTS

FOREWORD

I WELCOME this book as an account of charismatic revival as experienced by an Anglican priest who sees such revival not apart from but within the sacramental life of the Church. It is a book which will invite criticisms, some of which I share, and at the same time will do us the greater service of leading us to criticise ourselves about our awareness of the Holy Spirit and our response to Him.

There will be those who think, as I do, that it is misleading to use the word 'baptism' in describing a new and vivid experience of the Spirit, believing that we can be baptised only once. There will be those who think, as I do, that the gifts of an exciting kind are not necessarily the most significant for the Body of Christ amidst the variety of charismata described in 1 Corinthians 12 and of the harvest of the Spirit described in Galatians 5. The history of Christian saintliness will disallow the naming of particular gifts as a kind of criterion of spiritual reality.

Yet it cannot be denied that both in our teaching and in our experience the Holy Spirit has not been realised in the dynamic way which the first generation of Christians knew, and we must pray with a new confidence and expectancy, 'Come, thou Holy Spirit, come'. This book tells of the power of the Holy Spirit to create love, joy, self-sacrifice, power amongst Christians, and it cares for the variety of His gifts and for the common life of the Church. 'Isms' are man-made and divisive. Just as we need not 'sacramentalism' but the power of Christ in the sacraments, and not 'scripturalism' but the power of Christ in the scriptures, so we need not 'pentecostalism' but the disturbance of the Holy Spirit. This book will help us to be disturbed, and that is why I am deeply grateful to John Gunstone for writing it.

✠ MICHAEL CANTUAR:

PREFACE

THIS book describes what God is doing in his Church today through the charismatic movement, or pentecostalism as it is sometimes called (the small p signifies those teachings and practices associated with classical Pentecostalism which have been taken up by members of the established Churches).

I have, however, limited its scope to my own experience as an Anglican priest for two reasons. First, the subject is so vast that I had to be selective; and to select within the limits of what I have experienced myself seems sensible. Second, as a subject, pentecostalism needs personal testimony, for it is a way of life and a spirituality founded on the belief that the Holy Spirit can be known in love and power by the Christian now as in the apostolic age; and that kind of belief is best communicated first-hand.

So the book has grown out of what I have seen and heard over the last ten years. If the result is a patchwork—a page of theology, a paragraph of liturgy, a note on pastoral techniques, a personal story—that is because my experience of the charismatic movement has had a sort of patchwork effect. Pentecostalism crept into nearly everything that I did as a vicar and nearly everything that I was interested in as a Christian, until I realised that God the Holy Spirit was gently invading my life in a new way.

Until 1971 I was for thirteen years a parish priest in Romford on the eastern suburbs of London. The first chapter tells how, during those years, I was involved in the charismatic movement. Then I became chaplain of the newly-founded Barnabas Fellowship, a group of Christians who live as a community in Whatcombe House near Blandford, Dorset. Since I have been at Whatcombe, my experience of pentecostalism has widened considerably, not least in seeing how God established the community and led us into a ministry of the Spirit within his Church.

In the book I refer to a few of my former parishioners by Christian names and to four members of the community. The names of the parishioners have been altered to avoid embarrassment. The members of the community are Reg East, the warden, and his wife Lucia, and Ron Dodgson, the sub-warden, and his wife Jean. To them, to the rest of the Barnabas Fellowship, and to many other friends, I owe so much, as we have together sought God's will for us in these days of his Spirit's outpouring.

The editor of *The Franciscan* has kindly given me permission to use material on speaking in tongues which I contributed to his magazine (June, 1973).

Finally, I wish to thank Dr. Michael Ramsey for inviting me to write this book and for encouraging me to take as its subject my experience of the charismatic movement. It was a special privilege to receive this invitation from him because since the time when, as a student, I heard him preach and lecture at Durham, he has been for me one gifted by God to teach 'in demonstration of the Spirit and power.'

JOHN GUNSTONE

CHAPTER I

A PERSONAL PENTECOST

(i)

ONE spring morning in 1963 the telephone rang in the small house which served as a vicarage in the Romford parish where I was then priest-in-charge.

'Hello?' I said, picking up the receiver.

'Is that John Gunstone? You may not remember me—I'm Marion. We met in Mersea some months ago.'

I remembered her. She was a deaconess in a London parish, but her home was near Colchester, on Mersea Island where a friend, Reg East, was vicar.

'Yes?'

'What do you know about speaking in tongues?'

The question took me by surprise. It was the last thing I expected anyone to ask me over the telephone. Also, there was a note of anxiety in her voice which made me feel uneasy.

I struggled to recall the references to glossolalia I had half-noticed in the New Testament.

'Well, I don't think St. Paul was too keen on it,' I replied cautiously.

'But Reg is in the thick of it down in Mersea. Everybody's talking about it. I'm worried about him.'

I was mystified.

'What's he been doing?'

'I don't know any details, but I don't like the sound of it,' she went on. 'I rang you up because I thought you might be able to help him out of it.'

After she had rung off, I thumbed through the references to speaking in tongues in the Acts of the Apostles and 1 Corinthians and wondered how Reg could have become involved in a practice that was obviously part of the religious environment within which Christianity was born. The New English Bible calls glossolalia 'the gift of ecstatic utterance of different kinds'—and that was how I had regarded it: a refined form of emotional abandonment which disappeared when the Church became more orderly and civilised. I knew vaguely that the Pentecostalist Churches had revived the practice, but that was a whole Atlantic away from the worship of the Church of England!

I had known Reg since my college days. When he had been diocesan youth chaplain I had assisted him and his wife, Lucia, in summer holiday conferences for young people. He had been appointed to Mersea at about the same time that I had come to Romford, and we had kept in touch with one another. Reg had a heart-warming faith in God and an enthusiasm for his work as a priest, and it was not like him to be led astray by weird goings-on such as tongue-speaking.

Finally I decided to write to him—an inconsequential letter about nothing in particular, but at the end I mentioned casually that I'd heard he'd been speaking in tongues and said I hoped it improved his mastery of foreign languages. Back came a reply a few days later. Its tone was more serious than any letter I had received from Reg before. He said that he and Lucia were learning what remarkable things God was doing in his Church and they were trying to be led by the Spirit to understand the implications for the two of them.

The next four weeks took me through a series of events which seemed later to have been following a carefully-laid plan. I might have called them 'coincidences' once. Now I would call them 'God-incidences.' Looking back, I see how the Lord seized on my curiosity and used it to introduce me swiftly to what has come to be known as 'the charismatic movement', which was beginning to make its first impact on individual Christians in this country.

First, I went down to Mersea and learned from Reg and Lucia how they had been sent a magazine called *Trinity*, produced in California and printing stories of how Christians in different Churches were rediscovering the power of the

Holy Spirit in their daily lives. Speaking in tongues, interpretations, prophecies, healings, gifts of all kinds—it was as if the apostolic age of the Church was being revived in the twentieth century. I learned, too, that Reg had received the laying on of hands from two young Pentecostalists and had begun to speak in tongues when he prayed; Lucia had received the gift later. Reg said that they had never known the vitality of Christian faith in such a way before—and looking at him and his wife, I could believe that. I felt mildly envious of their obvious joy and confidence in the Lord.

Next, I was invited, as a member of the editorial committee of the *Essex Churchman,* to a press conference in the Gondoliers Room of the Savoy Hotel in London to meet Mrs Jean Stone, the editor of *Trinity.* Forty or so people crowded between walls decorated with scenes from the Gilbert and Sullivan opera—a fantastic setting for a strange story. Mrs Stone spoke to us with poise and assurance: Father Dennis Bennett, her Episcopalian parish priest, had received the baptism with the Holy Spirit, and members of his Californian congregation had launched the *Trinity* magazine to spread the news of what happened when people were touched by the Spirit. After the conference, I cornered the organizer, a certain Michael Harper, then curate of All Souls', Langham Place, and asked him to pray with me in tongues. He closed his eyes and whispered away in a strange language, and an odd sensation brushed over me. It was—spiritually uncanny. The heavy red colouring of the room—the liturgical colour of Pentecost —seemed curiously appropriate. Michael told me that he was leaving All Souls' to promote interest in the charismatic movement in Britain through the Fountain Trust, which he was establishing.[1] The Trust had arranged a mid-week conference at Stoke Poges on the gifts of the Spirit and he had one spare place. Would I like to come?

That was the third thing to 'happen' to me in that remarkable month. I attended the conference with a group of clergy and ministers from different denominations to listen to David du Plessis, a former secretary of the Pentecostal World Conference, as he expounded the work of the Holy Spirit in the

13

Church.[2] He had been attending the Second Vatican Council as an unofficial observer, and through what he said about the conversations he had had with Roman Catholic bishops and theologians in Rome, I realised how little I had known about the charismatic nature of the Body of Christ. Contrary to what I had imagined, the apostolic age of the Church had *not* passed! By the one Spirit we were all still living in it! I was thrilled! Over and over again I kept asking myself, Why hadn't I seen this before? There it was, calling to me out of the pages of the New Testament, expounded by the graceful Pentecostalist. It was at Stoke Poges that my curiosity about the charismatic movement was converted into a desire to receive the Holy Spirit more fully into my life. I was not clear what that meant! But I knew I wanted it!

And that led to the fourth and final 'God-incident.' I went back to Mersea and asked Reg to pray with me that I might be baptized with the Holy Spirit.

We were in the lounge of his vicarage. We sat facing one another and Reg prayed that the Lord would give me all that I desired. Then he stood behind my chair and laid his hands on my head, speaking in a strange tongue as he did so—an oriental-sounding language, beautiful in its cadences and consonants.

I moved my mouth hopefully.

Nothing happened.

I tried making a few sounds.

'Ah . . . Ugh . . . Ooomph . . . Ur . . .'

Still nothing happened.

'It's no good, Reg,' I gasped. 'I can't do it.'

He returned to his chair and sat looking at me for a while. I thought he looked disappointed. (He was, I discovered later, completely nonplussed. He had never laid hands on anyone before for the baptism with the Holy Spirit and he had no idea what he should do next.) Eventually he suggested that I should pray for the Spirit again when I was alone. I went home feeling perplexed and unworthy.

I received the Holy Spirit a few days later. I had finished saying morning prayer privately in church. Kneeling and

14

looking at the figures of Christ on the cross and of the Blessed Virgin Mary and St. John on the east wall, I was suddenly aware of the presence of God. I had only experienced his presence so dynamically on two or three previous occasions —when I kept a vigil before the altar of repose in the Community of the Resurrection's church at Mirfield during Holy Week, when I was ordained in Chelmsford cathedral. That morning I sensed the overshadowing of divine love like a warm cloak and I felt rising within me a longing to praise God with my whole being.

What could I say? The *Gloria?* Psalm 150?

Tongues . . . ?

The word 'Abracadabra' flitted into my mind. Ridiculous! That was a conjuror's mumbo-jumbo! Then I remembered that 'Abba' was the Aramaic for 'Father' and that the apostle had said, 'Because you are sons, God has sent the Spirit of his Son into our hearts, crying "Abba! Father!"' (Gal. 4:6).

Was that the way to begin?

Slowly I repeated the syllables, 'Abba . . ., Abba . . ., Abba . . .' Then, to my astonishment, my voice was guided into a flowing language and in my spirit I was caught up into God in a way I had never known before.

The joy of it was overwhelming. I wanted to laugh, cry, sing, all at the same time. The words came tumbling out and I knew I was praising God from the depths of my being, rejoicing in his love and goodness and salvation.

'I will magnify thee, O God, my King, and I will praise thy name for ever and ever.

Every day will I give thanks unto thee: and praise thy name for ever and ever' (Ps. 145:1–2).

The verses of the psalmist pealed through my mind as an accompaniment to the incomprehensible phrases I was uttering. Then a feeling of intense awe at the manifest power of God silenced me. I was very humble. Could that gift of tongues really have been meant for a lukewarm Christian like me?

I left the church building that morning with a peace in my heart that was far past my understanding. I could not explain

15

what had happened, but I knew that God had met me in a new way and blessed me.

But the implications of what he had done are still only slowly beginning to dawn on me.

(ii)

One of the first effects I noticed was that God became a reality in my life to an extent that I had not been conscious of before. Instead of the doubts and questionings that had plagued me as I wallowed in the wake of the theological radicalism of the early 'sixties, I now had an assurance of God's abiding presence that was peace-giving and strengthening. I do not mean that the problems of faith ceased entirely. After the initial pentecostal experience, I still had periods when God seemed far away from me. But the lasting effect was that I retained a remarkably firm conviction in the faithfulness of God, even in the midst of temptations to question the authenticity of the pentecostal experience itself.

An outcome of this was that I began to speak about 'God' and 'the Lord' and 'Jesus' more freely in my conversation without the sort of mild embarrassment that such references might once have caused me. When faced with a decision to make, I found myself asking, What does God want me to do? with a knowledge that I would be given the answer. When anything happened that I could not explain, I asked, What is God trying to say to me? Being more aware that God is in all things, and that he governs all events by his providence, I was learning to seek beyond the event to the Lord of history who stands behind it. The Lord seemed to have established himself more squarely in my life—and in spite of me!

Another effect was a slowly growing hunger for prayer, especially for corporate, informal prayer, where I could share needs and joys. For about three years this was not possible very often, for in spite of some interest in my parish, no one took the matter seriously enough to seek the baptism with the Spirit for themselves. I could only pray using the charism of tongues with others when I joined prayer meetings elsewhere. But then that changed. Two, three, then four parishioners received the Spirit and I was able to join them in a weekly charismatic prayer group.

I found I could take seriously Christ's promise, 'Whatever you ask in prayer, you will receive, if you have faith' (Mt. 21:22). I expected answers to prayers. I had often preached about such an expectation—in every sermon I had delivered on the subject—yet I had found it difficult to practise what I preached when I prayed myself. I continued to encounter —as I still encounter—the temptation to neglect my prayers; but the temptation seems to be more easily swept away, particularly when I pray in tongues and assemble with others for prayer.

Worship, too, became a joy rather than a burden. After ten years in the ordained ministry, the sense of privilege I had once had when I presided at a celebration of the eucharist or at evensong had worn off. Services had tended to become a performance, to be accomplished reverently but speedily—a duty undertaken for the benefit of others. Now I entered into the liturgy conscious that the Spirit which had inspired the words of the readings and prayers moved within me and within the congregation, uniting us with the whole Church on earth and heaven with the priestly intercession of Jesus Christ.

And yet another effect was a discovery of the Holy Spirit in the scriptures. I had always been interested in the Bible: I had used passages for meditation for years. But now the Word of God began to speak to me through its pages with a directness and an authority that I had not known before. Without setting aside what I had learned from commentaries and books, the texts of the Old and New Testaments became more precious for what they were in themselves rather than for the historical and critical problems that lay behind them. I have not become a fundamentalist, and I doubt whether I could ever be one; but my increased sensitivity to the Holy Spirit makes me more responsive to those inspired writings in which the Church has recognized the authoritative voice of God. My mind was illuminated by the scriptures and my faith was built up by them in a new way.

17

B

But the pentecostal experience left me with many puzzles. Could I speak about it as 'the baptism with the Holy Spirit' without ignoring all that the Spirit had done for me already through the Church? What did it mean in relation to my baptism, my confirmation and my ordination? What effect was it going to have on my life as an Anglican and as a priest?

I cannot say that I have been shown the complete answers to these puzzles and others like them, but nowadays they do not leave such big question-marks in my mind as they once did. In the last ten years the Lord has led me into a greater appreciation of what he is doing in his Church in our time. And since the fruit of the Spirit is so evident in much that I see, I am confident that theology will solve its own conundrums one day!

But we cannot neglect theology. The Holy Spirit is the Teacher of the Church. He leads us into all truth. So we must go on asking questions expecting to be enlightened—and in the next two chapters I shall sketch the sort of answers that I believe we can now give to two basic problems. When does the Christian receive the Holy Spirit? and, What justification is there for calling the pentecostal experience 'the baptism with the Holy Spirit'?

NOTES

[1] Michael Harper describes the beginnings of the charismatic movement in *As At The Beginning,* Hodder, 1965. His own involvement in it is told in his *None Can Guess,* Hodder, 1971.
[2] See David du Plessis, *The Spirit Bade Me Go,* Coverdale, 1971.

18

CHAPTER II

EACH HIS OWN GIFT

(i)

'REPENT, and be baptized every one of you in the name of Jesus Christ for the forgiveness of your sins; and you shall receive the gift of the Holy Spirit' (Acts 2:38).

Although the various traditions behind the New Testament describe the gift of the Spirit in different ways, they are one in their witness to the truth that when an individual turns to Jesus Christ in repentance and faith, he receives the Holy Spirit, as Peter told the crowd in Jerusalem on the day of Pentecost. To be a Christian is to be filled with the Spirit. All four gospels record John the Baptist's prophecy that when the Messiah came he would plunge his disciples into the life-giving power of God in the same way that he, the Forerunner, plunged them into the waters of the Jordan. In fact, John used the same word to designate that plunging: *baptizō*, to dip under, to swamp, to immerse completely. 'I have baptized you with water; but he will baptize you with the Holy Spirit' (Mk. 1:8). The fourth evangelist uses the present tense, 'he baptizes,' to indicate that the Spirit-baptism is a continuous act by Christ.

Paul's concept of the Holy Spirit was one of power—the dynamic power of God which, having raised Jesus from the dead, is now active in raising Christians from the death of sin: 'If the Spirit of him who raised Jesus from the dead dwells in you, he who raised Christ Jesus from the dead will give life to your mortal bodies through his Spirit which dwells in you' (Rom. 8:11). The practical implications of this are clear. When we become Christians, the Holy Spirit begins changing us. We are caught up into that renewal which the

Lord announced in the vision to the seer on Patmos: 'Behold, I make all things new' (Rev. 21: 5).

But there must be a desire on our part for change—or the beginnings of a desire. It was 'to the thirsty I will give water without price from the fountain of the water of life' (Rev. 21: 6). And yet even that desire is implanted by the Spirit. He opens our eyes to our sin and our need of salvation, for he 'convinces the world of sin' through the preaching of God's Word, 'the sword of the Spirit' (Jn. 16: 8; Eph. 6: 7). He brings us to faith in Jesus Christ as Saviour. We are treading on the old debate about God's will and man's free-will, but the Spirit is active in our creation as well as our redemption and the promptings that first turn us towards God must come from him. So the apostle could say that without the Spirit we have no claim to the title of Christian: 'Anyone who does not have the Spirit of Christ does not belong to him' (Rom. 8:9).

To be baptized with the Spirit is to be immersed in the transforming life of God. He makes effective in us all that has been achieved for us through the redeeming work of Jesus Christ. This is what the water signifies—a death to our old sinful lives and a resurrection to the new life in Christ. 'Do you not know that all of us who have been baptized into Christ Jesus were baptized into his death?' wrote Paul. 'We were buried therefore with him by baptism into death, so that as Christ was raised from the dead by the glory of the Father, we too might walk in newness of life' (Rom. 6: 3–4).

Paul saw the change which the Spirit brings to a Christian in terms of a transfiguration. To receive the Spirit is to enter into the new covenant, and this took the apostle back to the inauguration of the old covenant on mount Sinai and the giving of the law of God on the tablets of stone. 'You are a letter from Christ delivered by us,' he told the Corinthian Christians, 'written not with ink but with the Spirit of the living God, not on tablets of stone but on tablets of human hearts' (2 Cor. 3:3). And just as the glory of God was reflected in the face of Moses when he returned from mount Sinai, so also in a more permanent way the glory of God is reflected in the changed life of the Spirit-filled Christian: 'We all, with unveiled face, beholding the glory of the Lord, are being changed into his likeness from one degree of glory to another; for this comes from the Lord who is the Spirit' (2 Cor. 3:18). Through the Holy Spirit man is made new: 'If any one is in Christ, he is a new creation; the old has passed away, behold, the new has come' (2 Cor. 5:17).

In St. Luke John the Baptist's prophecy is that the Messiah will 'baptize you with the Holy Spirit and with fire.' The addition, 'with fire,' looks back to the Old Testament, where fire symbolized the purifying and empowering effect of God's presence—the burning bush, the theophany on mount Sinai, the acceptance of Elijah's oblation on mount Carmel, and the destruction of Ahaziah's messengers. Furthermore, the interval between the resurrection of Christ and the sending of the Holy Spirit in Acts is separated by the fifty days between the feast of Passover and the feast of Pentecost. The paschal setting of Christ's sacrifice interprets the redemptive work of God as the fulfilment for all mankind of that which was foreshadowed in the deliverance of Israel from Egypt. Luke, or his source, by associating the gift of the Spirit with the next great feast following the Passover in the Jewish calendar, underlined the truth that Pentecost crowned that redemptive work. Pentecost, fifty, is made up of seven times seven plus one: it symbolized completion (seven times the seven days of creation). The fifty days between the two Jewish feasts were regarded as days set aside by God for completing the grain harvest. Pentecost also commemorated the completion of the first stage of Israel's deliverance in the giving of the law on mount Sinai and the ratifying of the covenant.

In Acts, then, the fifty days between the resurrection and the giving of the Spirit form a dramatic interlude leading up to the climax of God's work in Jesus Christ. During the interval the resurrected Christ recalled for his disciples the promise that they would be baptized with the Holy Spirit, and on the fiftieth day the Spirit came in a theophany that resembled the giving of the law on mount Sinai: 'When the day of Pentecost had come, they were all together in one place. And suddenly a sound came from heaven like the rush of a mighty wind, and it filled all the house where they were sitting. And there appeared to them tongues as of fire, distributed and resting on each one of them. And they were all filled with the Holy Spirit and began to speak in other tongues, as the Spirit gave them utterance' (Acts 2:1–4).

The gift of the Spirit to the individual is associated more with the laying on of hands in Acts than with water-baptism. The Samaritan converts baptized by Philip received the Spirit when Peter and John came down to lay hands on them. Paul received the Spirit through the laying on of hands by Ananias before his baptism. The twelve disciples of John the Baptist at Ephesus also received the Spirit through the laying on of hands. But the pattern is not consistent. There is no reference to the laying on of hands at the baptism of the Ethiopian eunuch, and Cornelius and his household received the Holy Spirit before their baptisms. We must not read too much into these narratives, but at least they teach that the gift of the Spirit is not confined to the Church's sacramental signs.

The relationship between baptism in water and baptism with the Holy Spirit is close in the fourth gospel, so much so that to be baptized in water is to be made a new person in the Spirit: 'Truly, truly, I say to you, unless one is born of water and the Spirit, he cannot enter the kingdom of God' (Jn. 3:5). To desire Christ is to desire the life-giving water of the Spirit, and to receive the Spirit is to receive the life of God in such an abundance that it overflows from the individual towards others: 'On the last day of the feast, the great day, Jesus stood up and proclaimed, "If anyone thirst, let him come to me and drink. He who believes in me, as the scripture has said, 'Out of his heart shall flow rivers of living water.'"' Now this he said about the Spirit, which those who believed in him were to receive; for as yet the Spirit had not been given, because Jesus was not yet glorified' (Jn. 7:37–39).

It is not by chance that the Hebrew language expresses 'spirit' and 'wind' by the same concept, *ruach* (Greek, *pneuma*). Wind has a power that cannot be withstood or contained; moreover, it is mysterious and unpredictable in its comings and goings: 'The wind blows where it wills, and

22

you hear the sound of it, but you do not know whence it comes or whither it goes; so it is with everyone who is born of the Spirit,' Christ told Nicodemus (Jn. 3:8). Divine activity is the breathing of God: when the fourth evangelist expressed the gift of the Spirit in terms of Christ's breathing over his disciples, he was using the same basic image as Luke's description of the gift of the Spirit as like a strong gust of wind.

But, more than this, John saw the Spirit as the continuing presence of God among his people. As the Word of God was made flesh and tabernacled among the disciples, so the Holy Spirit, sent by the Father through the Son, continues that divine indwelling among those who are Christ's. He is 'another Counsellor' to teach and to lead us into all truth; he glorifies Christ by quickening our hearts and minds to the Gospel and by drawing us into a unity of love in Jesus. This is what the great prayer in chapter seventeen reveals: 'Father . . ., I glorified thee on earth, having accomplished the work which thou gavest me to do; and now, Father, glorify thou me in thy own presence with the glory which I had with thee before the world was made . . . Keep them in thy name, which thou hast given me, that they may be one, even as we are one . . . I do not pray for these only, but also for those who believe in me through their word, that they may all be one . . . The glory which thou hast given me I have given to them . . .'

Jesus Christ is glorified when in the Holy Spirit Christians are drawn to one another and love one another in obedience to his commandment. The change which the Holy Spirit works in us results in greater love for others. The primary effect of the gift of the Spirit, therefore, is love, the divine love of God overflowing from one to another as the principle of life on which the Christian community is established. This is a dominant motif throughout the New Testament. 'God's love has been poured into our hearts through the Holy Spirit which has been given to us' (Rom. 5:5).

To abide in the Spirit and to abide in love is one and the same thing in 1 John: 'By this we know that we abide in him and he in us, because he has given us of his own Spirit

23

. . . God is love, and he who abides in love abides in God, and God abides in him' (4: 13, 16).

Similarly, in the midst of his discussion on spiritual gifts, Paul firmly anchored what he said in the assertion that the greatest gift that the Spirit brings is love. Water, wind, fire—these are only signs to help us grasp the extent of the Spirit's activity. The truest manifestation of the Spirit given to us in this life is the love that Christians show to one another. To be baptized with the Spirit is to be immersed in the love of God.

(ii)

It follows from this that the gift of the Spirit and membership of the Church are closely interwoven with each other. Indeed, the Spirit is given through the Church as the Body of Christ for other members of the Church. We are not given the Holy Spirit for ourselves; we can never think of the gift of the Spirit as in any sense a personal possession or a mark of personal status. Rather, the Spirit seizes our isolated individuality and sets it within the fellowship of the Church. Our fulfilment as a person is discovered within the community of God's people: 'Like living stones be yourselves built into a spiritual house, to be a holy priesthood, to offer spiritual sacrifices acceptable to God through Jesus Christ' (1 Peter 2:5).

In Acts the disciples before the day of Pentecost are depicted as a group of associates, drawn together by the call of Jesus Christ. But the gift of the Spirit fused them into a new unity. They were 'all together in one place' (assembled for the unifying seal); they spoke as one of the mighty works of God; their tongue-speaking was—among other things—a prophetic sign that the disunity of Babel had been reversed. From this initial outpouring there emerged a Church in which the first Christians demonstrated their unity by the way 'they devoted themselves to the apostles' teaching and fellowship, to the breaking of bread and the prayers' (Acts 2:42).

In the old Israel the Spirit of God had been given to particular individuals, prophets, leaders, kings, psalmists, craftsmen. In the new Israel he is given to each member. Peter in his sermon of the day of Pentecost quoted the prophet Joel, 'I will pour out my Spirit upon all flesh,' to explain to the people in Jerusalem the meaning of what they saw and heard; 'all flesh' is qualified at the end of the quotation by the words, 'whoever calls on the name of the Lord' (Acts 2:16, 21).

The Holy Spirit comes to us through the Church because it is he who creates the Church and it is he who gives continuity to its fellowship, sustaining and guiding its members in their response to God. He is the principle of divine life which makes us one with each other. 'All who are led by the Spirit of God are sons of God' (Rom. 8:14). The universe was created by the Spirit through the word which God uttered at the beginning; the new creation is being brought into existence by the Holy Spirit, fulfilling in individuals the completed work of the Word of God made flesh.

The Spirit is manifested in the individual and in the Church through his 'gifts,' *charismata* or *pneumatika* which, according to Paul, are bestowed on each Christian according to the measure of his faith. I shall be discussing some of these gifts later in this book, but here I want to stress three things about them.

First, it is an error to divide a spiritual gift or charism from the Giver. A charism is not, as it were, a commodity or a power handed over by God to an individual, nor is the individual in any way the 'possessor' of a spiritual gift. A charism is the manifestation of God's activity in and through the words and acts of an individual Christian or a group of Christians. What is said and done is of God; the individual's or the group's part is simply obedience to God and faith in his purposes. The charism may be a natural ability transfigured by grace, so that a man who is 'generous by nature' (as we would say) reaches the point when in response to God he gives away all that he has. Or a charism may be supernatural, such as the working of miracles or prophecy (though we recognize that the boundary between what is natural and what is supernatural is sometimes difficult to distinguish). But it is essentially God's working through an individual in the power of his Spirit.

Secondly, charisms are given, not for the benefit of the recipient, but for the 'common good' (1 Cor. 12:7). By them the Church is 'edified' (1 Cor. 14:5). For Paul, as a man of the first century A.D., the task of building a palace, a fortress or a temple was enormous; it involved the labour of thousands toiling with the primitive equipment available in those days. So, too, the Holy Spirit equips the Church with his gifts for the enormous task of building up the Body of Christ. The author of Ephesians summed up the Pauline teaching on the charisms when he wrote, 'His gifts were that some should be apostles, some prophets, some evangelists, some pastors and teachers, for the equipment of the saints, for the work of ministry, for building up the body of Christ, until we all attain to the unity of the faith and of the knowledge of the Son of God, to mature manhood, to the measure of the statue of the fulness of Christ' (Eph. 4:11–13). The individual is himself sanctified by the Holy Spirit only inasmuch as he surrenders himself, as a changed person, to be used by God in this way. Pentecost fulfilled God's purposes in Christ for man; through the spiritual gifts God fulfils his purposes for each individual in the Body of Christ in a mutual ministry of love.

Thirdly, the charisms are for everyone. Every Christian is charismatic. 'To each is given the manifestation of the Spirit for the common good' (1 Cor. 12:7). 'As each has received a gift, employ it for one another, as good stewards of God's varied grace' (1 Pet. 4:10). Whoever has a share in the Spirit has a share in the spiritual gifts. Some charisms are temporary, others more permanent (for example, we shall distinguish shortly between *gifts* of healing for particular occasions and *the gift* of healing as a more or less continuous ministry); but they are for everybody according to God's will. They are not marks of special distinction belonging to a chosen few, whether on account of their enthusiasm or of their office in the Church, but they are a distinguishing mark of the whole Christian community.

26

After expounding the importance of the sacraments and the ordained ministry in the life of the Church, the Second Vatican Council declared:

'It is not only through the sacraments and Church ministries that the same Holy Spirit sanctifies and leads the people of God and enriches it with virtues. Allotting his gifts "to everyone according as he will" (1 Cor. 12: 11), he distributes special graces among the faithful of every rank. By these gifts he makes them fit and ready to undertake the various tasks or offices advantageous for the renewal and upbuilding of his Church, according to the words of the apostle, "The manifestation of the Spirit is given to everyone to profit" (1 Cor. 12: 7). These charismatic gifts, whether they be the most outstanding or the more simple and widely diffused, are to be received with thanksgiving and consolation, for they are exceedingly suitable and useful for the needs of the Church.'[1]

This reference—and others—to the charisms has prompted many Roman Catholic pentecostalists to see in the Council the first foreshadowings of the renewal movement which was to begin in their Church a few years' later (especially as Pope John XXIII, in one of his earliest public pronouncements about the forthcoming Council, had prayed for 'a new Pentecost' within the Church[2]). The reference owed its origins to a famous speech made in St. Peter's, Rome, during the Council by Cardinal Suenens, Archbishop of Malines-Brussels, 'On the Charismatic Dimension of the Church.' Years later, when asked in an interview if he knew that his speech would be regarded as a prophecy of the coming movement, he said:

'I didn't expect to make an intervention at that point at all. It was just the day before that I heard one of the other Cardinals proposing that the charismatic gifts were just for the early Church and not for today. I felt like I had to do something about that, because to deny the charisms seemed to undercut the possibility of a genuine awakening of the whole people of God, or at least to cloud the deepest significance of the fact that the Spirit is active and vital in each person. I asked a good biblical scholar to bring together all the important texts about charisms and I made an intervention with these as the basis. I concluded by saying that if the gifts of the Spirit are given like this, lay people must be invited to the Council, including women, for women are fully half the human race. . . . At that time I was not aware of the possibility of what we now see as the charismatic renewal developing, but if that intervention has been of use to the Holy Spirit in this way, so much the better.'[3]

NOTES

[1] *De ecclesia,* ii, 12, translated in Walter M. Abbott, *The Documents of Vatican II,* Geoffrey Chapman, 1966, p. 30. See the discussion in Gabriel Murphy, F.S.C., *Charisms and Church Renewal,* Catholic Book Agency, Rome, 1965, pp. 93ff.

[2] Text in Edward D. O'Connor, C.S.C., *The Pentecostal Movement in the Catholic Church,* Ave Maria Press, Notre Dame, Indiana, 1971, p. 287.

[3] Text of the interview in *New Covenant,* Vol. 2, No. 12, June 1973, p. 4.

CHAPTER III

BAPTIZED WITH THE SPIRIT

(i)

TEACHING about the Holy Spirit in the Church was, of course, familiar to me from theological textbooks, but after the pentecostal experience in 1963 the doctrine gradually became alive, as I saw evidence of the Holy Spirit's activity around me. It was the difference between seeing music on the printed page of the score and hearing it played by a full orchestra. The Spirit was a mysterious Person of the Blessed Trinity still, but no longer distant. I felt I had come to *know* him in a way that I had not known him before. Amazingly—when I consider what a failure I am as a Christian—he had come to dwell within me. 'It is no longer I who live, but Christ who lives in me' (Gal. 2:20) was a text that could describe what was beginning to happen in me!

Another text also spoke to me of total reliance upon God, not on myself, at that time:

'The Spirit of the Lord came upon Jahaziel . . . and he said, "Harken, all Judah and inhabitants of Jerusalem: Thus says the Lord to you, 'Fear not, and be not dismayed at this great multitude; for the battle is not yours but God's' "' (2 Chron. 20:14–15). I was beginning to 'let go and let God.'

But why had I to wait until I was thirty-six before I realised the fulfilment of Christ's promise to his disciples, 'You shall receive power when the Holy Spirit has come upon you' (Acts 1:8)?

Classical Pentecostalism has held firmly to the doctrine of a 'second blessing.' What it teaches is this: after conversion (and water-baptism), there remains another gift from God, associated usually with the laying on of hands, in which one receives the 'fulness' of the Holy Spirit and his divine indwelling. This is the Christian's personal 'Pentecost'—the equivalent of what the disciples experienced in the upper room. Some manifestation, usually speaking in tongues, is expected. Indeed, strict Pentecostalists demand it—'no tongues, no baptism with the Spirit.' After that, a person should realise increasingly in his life that he has been 'endued with power from on high,' power to witness for Christ. He will know that he is 'led by the Spirit,' and he will expect to receive spiritual gifts to perform all that is necessary as a follower of Jesus Christ, including the miraculous power to heal.

The concept of a 'second blessing' is difficult to accommodate to most theological traditions. The salvation offered by God in Jesus Christ is one. The idea that there is a two-stage means of entry into that salvation—with the corollary that there are two types of Christians, those who are Spirit-filled and those who are not—is based on one interpretation of a few Lucan texts; it does not witness to what the New Testament says as a whole on the work of the Holy Spirit in man.

On the other hand, the stress given by classical Pentecostalism to the Spirit's coming with power into the lives of individual Christians, plus the phenomenal success of the movement in winning people for Christ in areas where the missions of the established Churches have made little impact, have challenged us to scrutinize what we expect the Holy Spirit to do. When individuals like myself receive the 'baptism with the Holy Spirit,' we have to relate that experience to what we know of God's more familiar ways with us through the Church—through his Word, through our traditions of spirituality, through the sacraments, through the ordained ministry, and so on. In fact, as one brought up in the Anglo-Catholic wing of the Church of England, I found myself having to re-examine nearly every doctrine and practice that I had inherited.

(ii)

Christians who have had a conversion experience in their teenage or adult lives tell me that this is distinct from their subsequent pentecostal experience. They acknowledge, of course, that it was the Holy Spirit who brought them to repentance and faith, but they say that at their conversion he simply awakened in them a realisation of their sin and their need for the salvation which God offers in Jesus Christ. Their pentecostal experience took them on from this to an assurance of God's constant indwelling and power in their lives. We might describe the effect of the two experiences as a progress from all that Good Friday and Easter Day signify to all that Whitsunday signifies.

Here, perhaps, we have the beginnings of a solution to the problem. Christian initiation *is* our baptism with the Holy Spirit. But the totality of the saving act of God in Jesus Christ is so vast that Christian expectation and Christian practice have failed to contain the whole in view.

Liturgical scholars tell us that in the early Church water-baptism soon gathered to itself additional sacramental signs to indicate the reception of the Holy Spirit by the catechumen, notably the anointing with olive oil and the laying on of hands. The growth of the practice of infant baptism and the disintegration of the rites of initiation in the West led theologians to ascribe different aspects of the Spirit's activity to different sacramental signs—baptism to cleanse from sin, confirmation to strengthen for service—and to lose sight of what is implied in the promise, 'He will baptize you with the Holy Spirit.'

The centrality of the cross has dominated Western theology since medieval times—and rightly so, for it is the climax of God's mighty work for the salvation of mankind. But Calvary and the empty tomb are not the full Gospel. Paul wrote, 'I decided to know nothing among you except Jesus Christ and him crucified' (1 Cor. 2: 2); but later in the letter he went on to demonstrate the importance of the resurrection and the gift of the Spirit in redemption. Lucan chronology has shaped our Christian year so that we celebrate the ascension of Christ and the gift of the Spirit forty and fifty days respectively after our celebration of the cross and resurrection. We need to remember that in the fourth gospel's scheme of these saving events, Christ's first appearance to his disciples after his resurrection was also the occasion when he shared with them the glorious benefits of all that he had achieved for men through his passion—the forgiveness of sins and the breath of the Spirit. The crowning of Christ's redeeming work was not to be delayed by fifty days.

Confronted with the disintegration of the rites of initiation —the separation of baptism from confirmation, the former being administered in infancy, the latter being administered by a bishop years later—it is not surprising that medieval theologians in the West explained that baptism was primarily a sacrament of cleansing for a child born in original sin and that confirmation was a sacrament for the strengthening of the growing child in the Holy Spirit. They were, in fact, doing what the Pentecostalists were later to teach—looking for a 'second blessing.' The discussion on what confirmation might signify as a separate sacramental sign continues in our own times.[1]

However, two factors in Christian living and teaching have to be taken into account when we relate the pentecostal experience to our membership of the Church.

First, all that God desires to give us is present in Christian initiation. Baptism is the effective, sacramental sign of the forgiveness of our sins, our incorporation into the Body of Christ, the gift of the Spirit and eternal life itself. When we are initiated into the people of God we are 'sealed with the promised Holy Spirit, which is the guarantee of our inheritance until we acquire possession of it, to the praise of his glory' (Eph. 1:13–14). The New Testament does not teach anything less than that. To suggest, therefore, that there is anything lacking in the gift of God through baptism is to deny the teaching of scripture. We are initiated into the whole work of redemption, not just a part of it.

But, secondly, although all that God desires to give us is present in Christian initiation, his gift is only gradually appropriated by us through the years of our life, with many backslidings and failures. We have to 'take up our cross daily,' to 'die daily,' to be 'renewed every day'—the New Testament has a variety of expressions—and in this sense baptism is also a sign of what God will continue to do in us for the rest of our lives. We progress towards the kingdom of heaven among toils and tribulations; but they cannot divert us as long as we are in the Spirit. We know that 'God will supply every need of yours according to his riches in glory in Christ Jesus' (Phil. 4:19).

Bearing in mind this distinction between baptism as a sign of what God has done already for us and as a sign of what he is doing and will do, we can now begin to approach the term 'baptism with the Holy Spirit', avoiding the over-dogmatic interpretation which classical Pentecostalism has attached to the phrase.

If we are to be true to our Christian vocation, we must always be 'baptized with the Holy Spirit.' To be immersed in him is, as we have seen, the mark of being one with Jesus Christ in his Church. When we cease to live and move and think and talk outside the realm of the Spirit, we cease to be Christian. The texts quoted in the previous chapter reveal that the Holy Spirit is as essential to us in our spiritual life as the air we breathe is essential to us in our physical life; nothing less than that.

But it is quite consistent with this that there can be occasions in our Christian pilgrimage when the truth of what God does for us in Jesus Christ through the Holy Spirit is apprehended by us in a new and clearer way. The first of these occasions may arise when we reach a point of longing for spiritual renewal, for closer union with Jesus, for illumination of God's will, for power to witness to him. This may come when we encounter a crisis of need or of faith, when we plead for a knowledge of his presence and love. At such a moment we may make a decision for God which opens us to the gift of the Spirit—not in the sense that we have not received him before, but in the sense that we expose ourselves more to his influence than we have done before. Then God suddenly becomes more real, more powerful, more loving, more awe-inspiring; and from the depths of our inmost being we are aware that the Spirit is lifting us up in

33

C

Christ towards the Father. At such a moment God may well manifest himself in our lives by the bestowal of a new charism; and that experience could be, as far as we are concerned, an entering into what it means to be 'baptized with the Holy Spirit.'

In an interesting discussion on pentecostalism and traditional spirituality, Fr. Edward O'Connor points out that the classical doctrine of the presence of God has always recognized that, through the gifts of faith and love, the Christian can be brought closer to God—that is, made more aware of his abiding presence. 'This is a point on which the pentecostal spirituality corresponds so perfectly with the great perspectives and promises of this classical doctrine that it gives reason to ask whether our usual practice today has not fallen short of our own authentic tradition.' A moment when the presence of God becomes more real is never, of course, referred to as 'the baptism with the Holy Spirit' in the spiritual writers of the past, but they knew the experience. For them it was the normal and typical effect of the inspirations and gifts of the Holy Spirit. 'Only when Christ reveals himself to us by the Spirit are we placed in his presence in a way that opens a new dimension in our lives and pierces us to the heart, so that we cry, "Rabboni!" However, this gift and revelation are meant to come to us all.'[2]

(iii)

If theology and experience went hand-in-hand, I should expect individuals to experience 'the baptism with the Holy Spirit' at the same time as they were given the sacrament of Christian initiation. This would give a greater note of authenticity to phrases in the rites such as:

Grant that in baptism these thy servants may be made his members by thy Holy Spirit . . .

Bless . . . this water, that all who are baptized in it . . . may know the power of his resurrection, and may walk in newness of life . . .

Send forth upon them thy Holy Spirit . . .

Defend, O Lord, these thy servants that they may . . . daily increase in thy Holy Spirit more and more . . .

I have known people who, baptized as adults in the Baptist Church, began speaking in tongues as they came up from the font, with all the signs of a pentecostal experience, because they were taught beforehand to expect an anointing of the Spirit.

But for many reasons this has not happened to most of us. We sometimes wait years before repentance and faith lead us to a fuller commitment to Jesus Christ and the power of the Spirit—often not until our repentance and faith have been tested in the fire of Christian witness and ministry. Then we realize how much more we depend on the gift of the Spirit than when we first believed.

The analogy of Israel's liberation from Egypt, with years of wandering in the desert before the ratification of the covenant, is a powerful one in terms of Christian spirituality. The journey from the Red Sea to Sinai can be a long one. During it the people of Israel murmured and were disobedient. They turned from the worship of God to the worship of an idol. They were punished. Yet, even so, they were 'all under the cloud' (the symbol of the divine presence) 'and all passed through the sea, and all were baptized into Moses' (as a 'type' of Christ) 'in the cloud and in the sea' (1 Cor. 10: 1–2). God did not reject them as his people, but in the end brought them into his promised land and among them founded his holy city.

The phrase 'the baptism with the Holy Spirit' is, therefore, full of meaning when it is applied to a pentecostal experience by the person concerned. For it describes a fulfilment in his life of what the sacrament of baptism promised, namely, a new encounter with God through the power of the Spirit which opens the Christian's eyes to the truth of what Christ meant when he said to his disciples, 'You shall see greater things than these' (John 1:50). I shall continue to use the phrase 'the baptism with the Holy Spirit' in this book (though without the inverted commas) on the understanding that it refers to this experience.

NOTES

[1] The matter has been aired recently in *Crisis for Confirmation*, ed. Michael Perry, S.C.M. Press, 1967.
[2] Edward D. O'Connor, *op. cit.*, pp. 199 and 201.

CHAPTER IV

SPEAKING IN TONGUES

(i)

NOTHING in the charismatic movement causes more perplexity and misunderstanding than the gift of tongues. To those who have not received the charism it can be amusing, irritating or even repulsive when their friends talk about it. The non-glossolist feels that he is being treated as a second-rate Christian because he doesn't 'have it', or he has the suspicion that his friends are being sadly misled by their emotions. Soon after I had received the baptism with the Spirit I went to a priest whose spiritual discernment and common sense I respected and described to him what had happened to me. His face became grave as he listened, and when I had finished speaking he earnestly warned me to give up the practice.

Glossolists are generally enthusiastic about the charism; they are conscious that from the time they began praying in tongues their devotional life was enriched and their faith was slowly built up. The apostle's statement that 'he who speaks in a tongue edifies himself' (1 Cor. 14:4) is certainly borne out by those who are being baptized with the Spirit and receiving the gift of tongues today. They experience forms of praise and adoration of God which were rarely theirs before.

Speaking in tongues is a gift of prayer—this is the chief point to be recognized. Its scriptural basis is not disputed. In Acts it is a means whereby the apostles proclaimed the mighty works of God and magnified the Lord. Paul's letter to the Church in Corinth indicates that, although he knew of the dangers of uncontrolled glossolalia, he himself spoke in tongues more than any of his readers and he wanted them all to use this kind of prayer. The reference in Romans 8: 26–27 is more problematic. Certainly when I wish to intercede for a person I sometimes pray in tongues, especially when I have a particular concern and I am not sure how to express it in words: this seems to me to be one of the things which Paul meant when he wrote, 'We do not know how to pray as we ought, but the Spirit himself intercedes for us with sighs too deep for words. And he who searches the hearts of men knows what is the mind of the Spirit, because the Spirit intercedes for the saints according to the will of God.' But New Testament scholars are not agreed on what the apostle was referring to, and so the meaning of the text is open.

It is argued that the charism was not important to Paul because he placed it last on his list of spiritual gifts in 1 Cor. 12:4–11, because he said although he wanted them all to speak in tongues he wanted them to prophesy even more, and because he remarked that when he prayed in a tongue his mind remained unfruitful. Yet a straightforward reading of 1 Cor. 14–16 does not leave me with that impression. The apostle was not trying to prevent the Corinthian Christians from speaking in tongues; he was encouraging them to use the charism in a proper, orderly way. There were occasions when speaking in tongues in public was disruptive. Then the glossolist must use his gift in private prayer. But when someone spoke in tongues in an assembly of the local Church, then the congregation should wait for an interpretation through which all could be edified. Both prayers in a known language and prayers in tongues had their rightful function in Christian devotion: 'I will pray with the spirit and I will pray with the mind also' (1 Cor. 14:15).

Psychological studies of speaking in tongues have produced varied results. Those who are sympathetic to the charismatic movement, like Morton T. Kelsey, accept glossolalia as a significant psychological and religious phenomenon, best understood in relation to Carl Jung's theory of the collective unconscious: in this view speaking in tongues is an invasion into the conscious of those deep areas of the human psyche where the Spirit of God touches the spirit of man. Less sympathetic observers, like John P. Kildahl, conclude that

38

glossolalia can be learned almost as any other ability can be learned, and that whether one calls the practice a gift of the Spirit is a matter of individual choice. Since Dr. Kelsey and Dr. Kildahl are (or were when they wrote their books) both non-glossolists themselves, it is interesting that they agree on two points: (1) that no one can truly evaluate an experience that he has not had himself, and (2) that from a psychological point of view, tongue-speaking seems almost always to have been beneficial in helping those who practised it towards a greater integration of their personalities.[1]

The gift of tongues—and all that stems from it in a greater awareness of the Holy Spirit's presence in the Church and of the charismatic nature of Christian living—seems to be one of the means by which God is asserting the sovereignty of his Word in the midst of his over-analytical and over-rationalistic people. From a human point of view glossolalia is foolishness: grown men and women earnestly uttering sounds that they do not understand. It is certainly embarrassing to have to admit to your sceptical friends that you use glossolalia in your prayers! But speaking in tongues is a form of prayer that compels us to set aside the operation of our intellect and allow our speech-mechanism to free-wheel, as it were, believing that God will guide and accept the sounds that we make as a language of praise to him.

Dennis Bennett wrote, 'It would seem that the faculty of speech . . . is the main thing that obstructs the freedom of the Holy Spirit in the believer's life. It is the focus of our intellectual pride. A neurosurgeon friend made this interesting comment one day: "I understand why God uses speaking in tongues. The speech-centres dominate the brain. I don't see how God could do much about the physical brain unless he got hold of the speech-centres." '[2]

'In speaking in tongues,' said Simon Tugwell, 'we surrender one little limb to God's control. Ideally, this should help us more and more to make ourselves over to him, gradually dispossessing ourselves of ourselves, until finally he is our all in all, the centre of our motivation, the source and goal of all that we are and do. . . . The way to get through the fog of thought is to sink to a deeper level than thought or desire. The Greek Fathers recommended that we should turn to the prayer of the heart, reciting the prayer of Jesus ("Lord Jesus Christ, Son of God, have mercy on me") without thoughts. But tongues is even more precisely the tool for the job. . . . It reaches beyond ourselves and our dilemma; in it the finger of God can reach down, through our thoughts and conflicting desires, to that deeper level, where both thoughts and desires can be modulated and transformed, so building us up on the Rock which is Christ.'[3]

(ii)

Speaking in tongues, then, engages the depths of our personalities, far beyond the bounds of the conscious, in devotion and commitment to God. 'We have received not the spirit of the world,' wrote Paul, 'but the Spirit which is from God, that we might understand the gifts bestowed on us by God. And we impart this in words not taught by human wisdom but taught by the Spirit, interpreting spiritual truths to those who possess the Spirit' (1 Cor. 2: 12–13). The apostle was not specifically referring to speaking in tongues in this passage (he was urging that 'the word of the cross' should be preached in the inspiration of the Holy Spirit, not in reliance upon subtle arguments); but it is nevertheless true that those of us who use glossolalia in our prayers have been led to understand 'the gifts bestowed on us by God' in a far profounder way than we would have understood them if we had no personal experience of this charism. The spiritual gift of tongue-speaking triggers off a greater awareness of the charismatic nature of our Church membership and so can lead to a greater desire in us to serve God in the power of the Holy Spirit—if we have not fallen into the error of seeking the gift of tongues solely for the experience itself (that is one of the constant dangers of the charismatic movement).

'One who speaks in a tongue speaks not to men but to God; for no one understands him, but he utters mysteries in the Spirit' (1 Cor. 14: 2). Tongues is not an ecstatic language or an utterance without meaning: it is a devotional communication with God. The Greek words used to designate it are *dialektos* and *glossa*, words which refer to conversation, discourse or talking, not gibberish. I was puzzled how the sounds which I uttered—and which, as I practised using them, became more fluent and rhythmic—could possibly represent another language without my learning a vocabulary and a grammar. David du Plessis pointed out to me at Stoke Poges it has been calculated that there have been at least six thousand seven hundred languages in the world, many of them with regional variations in dialect. It is not therefore difficult to believe that God will guide the sounds I make into the words and phrases for his own purposes. It is, I think, the element of faith required in this form of prayer which leads to a greater faith in the other works of God through the inspiration and empowering of the Holy Spirit.

Glossolalia is occasionally recognized as a language by someone who knows the language or whose native tongue it is. Books on the charismatic movement and speaking in tongues classify various instances of this. The most remarkable example I have ever come across was told me by Pastor S. D. Barnabas of Mysore City. He had been invited to address evangelistic rallies in another part of India each night for a week. For the first two evening meetings he spoke through an interpreter, for he did not know the local language, but on the third evening he turned up at the meeting to find that the interpreter was ill and that there was no one else who was sufficiently fluent in both languages to translate for him. So, with a prayer to the Lord for help, he mounted the podium and addressed the crowd in a manner that he usually reserved for praying in tongues. The crowd listened in silence for an hour and a quarter. Afterwards, he was asked why he had used an interpreter on the previous two evenings, for they had understood what he was saying to them!

People sometimes ask whether the language changes as one prays. I think it does, but it is not an easy question to answer, because when I am praying in tongues I do not listen

41

very attentively to what I am saying. My mind is usually turning towards God or towards the person I am praying for. When I begin to pray in tongues, I nearly always experience an inner peace and an awareness of God's presence, similar to the initial experience in 1963, and I end with a feeling that the prayer has been accepted by God because it was his prayer, anyway, and not mine.

I often pray in tongues quietly in preparation for a ministry—before a sermon, before counselling, when I am making a pastoral visit, prior to laying on hands for someone to ask God to bless them in a need. Then I experience a sensation of reaching out towards the person or the group as I do so—a sensation that is akin to love. Even a person whom I am not particularly attracted to, or whom I tend to avoid by natural instinct, becomes quite important in my estimation as I pray. Any prayer would do this, I know, but the point of praying tongues for a person is that you do not have to think of words with which to express the prayer—words which might be affected by your natural attitude towards him.

A woman once asked me to pray for the healing of her arthritis. Earlier in the day she had questioned me about tongue-speaking and reacted against it rather sharply. I had felt slightly alienated from her and her request came as a surprise. As I laid hands on her, the thought flashed through my mind that if I prayed quietly in tongues for a few moments before praying aloud in English—my usual custom, as I have explained—I might antagonize her. But I decided to proceed as usual and prayed in tongues which she could hear before I went on to ask God to heal her. Later, she came to me and said, 'While you were praying in tongues, I heard the Lord say, "This is the language I use." ' There was no longer any alienation in me!

Should all Christians expect to pray in tongues? Because the charism has led me to recognize more clearly what God is doing in our time, my instinctive answer to that question is, Yes, certainly; but I have to face two facts. First, the Holy Spirit has worked and is working so powerfully in the lives of many non-glossolist Christians (and they are so obviously

42

used by him far more effectively than I can ever be) that I have to admit that it does not seem to be an essential spiritual gift in every case. Secondly, a small number of people have sincerely desired the gift for many years and not been granted it. Paul may have said, 'I want you all to speak in tongues,' and 'I thank God that I speak in tongues more than you all'; but he also said, 'Do all speak with tongues?'—expecting the answer, No (1 Cor. 14:5; 14:18; 12:30). Glossolalia is a means of release in the Spirit for many Christians, but others find release in God in other ways and through other charisms. My considered answer to the question, therefore, is the same as that which used to be given by Anglo-Catholics when asked whether or not everybody should go to confession: all may, some do, others should.

(iii)

So far I have only discussed praying in tongues as a means of private devotion for personal edification. For two or three years this was the only way I used it, for I was rarely in the kind of group where I could pray in tongues aloud; but as other members of the congregation were baptized with the Spirit, I joined in their prayer group and we were led to speak in tongues and to interpret.

In his instructions to the Church in Corinth, Paul ranked prophesying a more valuable charism for public worship than tongues 'unless some one interprets, so that the Church may be edified.' The purpose of the spiritual gifts is their use within the Christian community so that others may be encouraged and built up. Tongues are only to be used when the exercise of the gift leads to an interpretation so that others may share in the charism. Paul was quite specific about this: 'If any speak in a tongue, let there be only two or at the most three, and each in turn; and let one interpret. But if there is no one to interpret, let each of them keep silence in church and speak to himself and to God' (1 Cor. 14:27–28).

The prayer group in my parish had met for several weeks and we had spoken in tongues quietly in the midst of other

43

devotions. The mysterious sounds that came from our lips were thrilling but hardly edifying. We knew that until the gift of interpretation was given to someone in the group, we would advance no further in this kind of prayer. But who was to take the first step? How did one receive the charism of interpretation? In those days charismatic prayer groups were comparatively rare and we had little experience of the exercise of the spiritual gifts in them.

One evening a member of the group was praying in tongues more boldly than usual—a beautiful lyrical sound that lilted like music—when I was suddenly aware of words forming in my mind. I do not remember now what they were, but I do remember that they did not add up to an intelligible sentence. I assumed they were a distraction and tried to ignore them. But they would not be moved. Instead, they began stringing themselves into a sentence—but not, as far as I could tell, a sentence that I was deliberately composing like the one I am writing now. With some hesitation—I was afraid I might make a fool of myself in the midst of a devout moment—I started saying them aloud.

The voice was mine, but what I said was not the sort of thing that I would normally have said in extemporary prayer. I had the definite impression that I was being used by the Spirit to communicate to the people sitting around me. It was an awesome experience.

Then I was conscious that the group was listening intently. My concentration vanished. I faltered over a word, and stopped.

I opened my eyes. They were staring at me.

'John, why did you stop?'

'It—it wasn't me!'

'We knew it wasn't! But it was wonderful! The Lord was speaking so clearly. . . . You should have gone on.'

An interpretation is not a translation of a tongue; it is an explanation or an expounding of the charism to others (this is what the Greek word *diermēnuo* means). It can take the form of a prayer for divine assistance, an act of dedication, a statement of faith and assurance, an expression of praise

44

and adoration as well as words of edification, exhortation and comfort. Sometimes an interpretation can be an answer to the prayer, praise and statement of faith which has been made in a tongue; in that case it would be more accurate to call it a prophecy (which we will discuss in the next chapter). But we do not have to be too technical in our definitions. When the interpretation is given in the power of the Holy Spirit it can be an enormous comfort to those in the group for whom it is addressed.

On a number of occasions God has used a gift of interpretation to strengthen and encourage me through another in a prayer group, usually when that person was quite unconscious that I was the one who was being blessed. And I have begun to learn how to speak out in faith when an interpretation has been given to me.

Interpretations come in various forms. Recently I was leading a large prayer meeting in a parish at the beginning of a weekend conference. Someone started speaking in tongues. As I listened, I was conscious of an increasing heaviness about my arms and legs that crept over my whole body. I felt as if I was strapped to the chair. When the glossolalia ceased, I wondered if I should describe this sensation to the meeting, but then it suddenly came to me that I should speak God's assurance that heaviness would be lifted. The words came to me fluently: they were to the effect that, although we were weighed down so much that it seemed impossible to lift our hands in prayer and to step out with our legs along the pathway of faith, yet God would release us.

The heaviness left me as I spoke. The prayer meeting continued in a lively manner. After it was over, a small group came to me and thanked me for the interpretation.

'We were expecting God to do so much this weekend, but we all felt heavy with despair when we came to the meeting. Now the heaviness has gone since God spoke through you. We know we're going to be greatly blessed during the next two days.'

They were!

Whatcombe itself owes much to an interpretation. One day

in 1966 a prayer group met in Mersea vicarage. It consisted of Reg East, Lucia, and a few friends. Someone spoke in a tongue and an interpretation was given. The interpretation said that within a fortnight the Easts would meet at a conference the couple who would join them in a project they already had in mind of forming a small community to run a conference centre.

Just over a week later the Easts were acting as host and hostess at a Fountain Trust conference at High Leigh in Hertfordshire. As the days went by they forgot about the interpretation, and it was not until Reg had seen the last guest out of the hall at the end of the conference that he suddenly remembered it. The couple had not appeared after all!

Unknown to him, however, a man and his wife were at that moment driving away from the house with an uneasy thought in their minds that they ought to have spoken to Reg before they left.

Ron Dodgson, a heating engineer from Manchester, said to Jean: 'I think the Lord wants us to go back and speak to Reg.'

'I think he does, too,' said Jean.

Ron turned the car round and drove back to High Leigh. Feeling a little foolish, they went back into the entrance hall and saw Reg clearing up some papers.

'We've come back to say good-bye,' explained Ron awkwardly.

Reg looked at them for a moment, and then went to find Lucia. He told her two people had come back to speak to him and he felt he ought to tell them about their projected community. She agreed, and they went to see the Dodgsons in the hall.

At the beginning of July 1971 the Easts and the Dodgsons arrived at Whatcombe House together as co-founders of the Barnabas Fellowship.

What would have happened if that member of the prayer group in East Mersea vicarage had not spoken out in faith the interpretation the Holy Spirit had given him?

People ask, 'How can I speak in tongues?' This is the wrong question. The right one is, 'How can I receive the Holy Spirit more fully into my life so that I can love the Lord and serve him in others more effectively?' We should seek God first; the charisms come later. Simon Magus' error was that he sought the power of the Holy Spirit without first committing himself wholly to Jesus Christ.

When we have asked the right question, the answer is fairly straightforward. First, we make an act of repentance—either privately to God, or by making our confession to a priest. It is important, when we do, that we should renounce utterly any connection we may have had with the occult, spiritualism, or practices of a related kind. In fact, a person who has been involved in these things should seek the ministry of a priest or a layman who is experienced in counselling in such matters.

Next, we ask Jesus Christ to fill us with the Holy Spirit. We may do this quietly on our own, but it often helps if we do it in the presence of others who are praying with us. Our petition is then supported by our fellow-members in the Church.

Then, as we offer ourselves anew to God at the end of the prayer, we may experience an inexplicable but overwhelming assurance that the Lord has come to us afresh in love and power. We may want to say, 'Thank you, Jesus!' We may want to laugh, to weep, or to shout out, 'Alleluia!' And we may wish to praise God so fervently that the English language seems inadequate: at such a moment the gift of tongues is frequently given.

But it may be that the charism does not immediately manifest itself. What should we do then? We should wait—full of hope. 'If you then, who are evil, know how to give good gifts to your children, how much more will the heavenly Father give the Holy Spirit to those who ask him' (Luke 11: 13). The Holy Spirit is given in answer to prayer. Even if he does not immediately manifest himself in tongues, he will demonstrate his indwelling in some other way. Our friends can commend us to God in the words of the author of Hebrews. 'May the God of peace, who brought again from the dead our Lord Jesus, the great shepherd of the sheep, by the blood of the eternal covenant, equip you with everything good that you may do his will, working in you that which is pleasing in his sight, through Jesus Christ' (13:20-21).

(v)

The gift of tongues can be used in worship in what is called 'singing in the Spirit.' Someone in the group begins to sing using their tongue and allowing the tune to come spontaneously; others take it up in their own tongues, until a hymn of praise wells up in a glorious symphony of sound, blending together, softer, louder, until it dies away as mysteriously as it came, leaving an unforgettable atmosphere of devotion. Singing in the Spirit is a glorious accompaniment to the *Sanctus* and the acclamations in the eucharist, and as a post-communion devotion.

NOTES

[1] Morton T. Kelsey, *Speaking with Tongues,* Epworth Press, 1964; John P. Kildahl, *The Psychology of Speaking in Tongues,* Hodder, 1972.
[2] Dennis and Rita Bennett, *The Holy Spirit and You,* Coverdale, 1971, p. 61.
[3] Simon Tugwell, *Did you receive the Spirit?* Darton, Longman and Todd, 1971, p. 70

CHAPTER V

LET THE PROPHETS SPEAK

(i)

BELIEF that the Holy Spirit would control the voice of an ordinary Christian in the direct manner required for interpreting a tongue was hard for me to accept. When I allowed myself to be used for an interpretation, or when I listened to someone else being used, I constantly had to struggle with the nagging doubt, Are we making it up? But an answer to the question became more urgent when we began to seek the gift of prophecy.

Prophecy is an utterance given by the Holy Spirit that can take the form of an exhortation, an encouragement, a prayer, a canticle, or a song. There may even be a prediction channelled through this charism which God wants to speak to others, or it may present some aspect of God's revelation of himself that we are unaware of or that we have been neglecting. In other words, when we seek the gift of prophecy we are seeking to become God's mouthpiece! And to me that seemed a highly risky and dangerous business! Who was I to assume that God would want to use me in this way? Surely he would only use very special people for exercising such an important function in the Church?

When asked by Joshua to prevent the prophesyings of Eldad and Medad, Moses cried out, 'Would that all the Lord's people were prophets, that the Lord would put his spirit upon them' (Numbers 11: 29). And Joel certainly saw the new age as one in which prophecy was a charism which would be shared by all, young as well as old, not just a chosen few:

49

D

'And it shall come to pass afterward,
that I will pour out my spirit on all flesh;
your sons and your daughters shall prophesy,
your old men shall dream dreams,
and your young men shall see visions.
Even upon the menservants and maidservants
in those days, I will pour out my spirit'

(Joel 2 : 28–29).

At Pentecost Peter claimed that this prophecy had been fulfilled, through the outpouring of the Holy Spirit; and in the apostolic Church we see the charism of prophecy widely used in an occasional way, as in the case of the four daughters of Philip, and in a more continuous manner that qualified the one so gifted to the semi-official title of 'prophet', like Agabus. The office of a prophet may well have been a permanent reminder to the whole Church of its prophetic ministry as the offices of pastor and elder have been permanent reminders to the whole Church's pastoral and priestly ministry in the name of Christ.

The Church has generally seen the exercise of the gift of prophecy in those of her members whose vocation it is to preach and to write about the Christian faith. Like the Israel of old, we have tended to restrict the use of the term 'prophet' to men and women who have been outspoken in what they believed God was saying to their generation. Occasionally we have also heard God speak through a fellow-Christian's manner of life or gifted ministry to others. In more recent years, thanks to the witness of classical Pentecostalism, we are learning that many Christians can minister with a charism of simple prophecy to bring to one another the living promises of God. Building the Church upon the foundation of the prophets as well as the apostles can be interpreted as a continuous activity of the Holy Spirit among the people of God, not one that was confined to the first century A.D.

As I said, I found the charism of prophecy difficult to accept as authentic at first because of my suspicions of self-deception and my fears of manipulation. But slowly I came to realise that for years I had accepted the fact that the Holy

Spirit had used me to communicate God's Word unexpectedly and directly. There were the sermons in which I had been prompted to say things that I could not have prepared, the prayers which came to me in moments of crisis when ministering as a priest, the verse of scripture or the apt sentence which came through my fingers to the typewritten manuscript paper without any conscious working of my mind. I had no difficulty in hearing God speak through these instances. Why, then, should I hesitate to believe that the Spirit could speak through me if I offered myself in humility and faith to be used as his mouthpiece in ministry to another?

I came to realise, too, that God does not set aside our personalities, our education, our ways of expressing ourselves, when he ministers through us in interpretation and prophecy. He uses them, but he uses them in a transfigured way. Prophecy is an outward and audible sign of the inward presence of God's Spirit within us. For example, if I hear Ron speaking a prophecy, I am not just listening to Ron's voice being used in an automatic way that makes him an impersonal instrument; I am hearing him speaking with his normal dialect, phraseology and vocabulary, but inspired by God in such a way that Ron's words are the means through which I learn God's will for me.

What convinced me in the end was when I was the subject of a number of ministries of interpretation and prophecy which brought God's grace to me in power. I shall always remember one prayer meeting when someone who knew nothing about me but my name was prompted to walk over to my chair, lay his hands on my head, and pronounce a prophecy. His words were for me the words of our Lord himself, assuring me and encouraging me in a particular situation (about which the man himself could have known nothing) that every problem was in the divine hands. From that time my doubts and difficulties about this form of ministry dissolved. God had used this man to impart to me a spiritual gift to strengthen me, and I realised what a wonderful charism this can be for the building up of the Church.

Shortly before we opened Whatcombe as a conference

centre, I was moved to speak a short prophecy. Reg happened to have a pencil and paper in his hand at the time, and he scribbled the prophecy down:

'As my Word became flesh in my Son,
  so must my Word become flesh in you.
When you speak, I am to speak;
When you love, my love is to embrace those whom you love;
Let my Word live in you,
  that you may become my living words.'

It was not the kind of statement I would have made up for myself—not even, I believe, if I was trying to write a meditation. Looking at the words in print now (I had put the piece of paper on which Reg scribbled them in a file and forgotten all about it until I happened to find it one day while I was making notes for this book) I can hardly believe that they came from my lips. But at the time they were uttered they spoke to us as a community about our vocation and ministry to other members of the Body of Christ.

(ii)

'Let two or three prophets speak, and let the others weigh what is said' (1 Cor. 14: 29). 'Do not despise prophesying, but test everything' (1 Thess. 5:20–21). When we listen to a prophecy, even of the simplest kind, we must judge if it is from the Lord. We must reject it if it comes from the human imagination or from the devil. 'The prophets are prophesying lies in my name; I did not send them, nor did I command them or speak to them. They are prophesying to you a lying vision, worthless divination and the deceit of their own minds.' The warning which the Lord gave through Jeremiah (14: 14) applies just as much today. This is why it is important in a prayer meeting to have a pause after an interpretation or a prophecy has been given to enable the group to consider what has been said.

Anything prophesied which is contrary to scripture is immediately suspect; so is anything contrary to the Church's teaching. 'By this you know the Spirit of God: every spirit which confesses that Jesus Christ has come in flesh is of God, and every spirit which does not confess Jesus is not of God' (1 Jn. 4, 2–3). When a prophecy is made concerning a doctrinal matter which is under debate it should be treated circumspectly. (Among the hundreds of interpretations and prophecies which I have heard, I have never been aware of one that came into this category, but the warning should be made.) Prophecies which tell us to do something which seriously affects our lives should be regarded with caution and carefully examined. If they are of God they will be confirmed in another way, through what someone else says or through guidance in answer to prayer. I have received letters which read, 'The Lord has told me that you are to come and address a meeting at such a place on such a date . . .'! My diary confirmed that the Lord wanted me to be somewhere else!

On the other hand, a spirit of scepticism can rob the ministry of interpretation and prophecy of its edifying assistance, and if we adopt a suspicious attitude towards every manifestation of these charisms, then we shall never hear the Lord speaking to us. A group of Christians who are growing together in the Spirit of God, and who are learning to trust one another in love, should seek the charism of discernment with confidence. Anyone who prophesied falsely in that kind of fellowship would soon be convicted of his error. The only prophesies which did not witness in truth to me (and I cannot remember more than one or two) were given in large meetings where the person who spoke was hidden in anonymity. When a prophecy is given, we should thank God for his goodness in speaking to us and meditate on what was said. If it does not seem to apply to us personally, we should assume that it is spoken for someone else's benefit.

Paul stressed the importance of the gift of prophecy. He wanted all his Corinthian congregation to exercise the charism. Prophecy enables God to meet hidden needs in individual Christians and in groups. True prophecy, endued with divine life and power, reaches out to strengthen, to encourage and to stabilize members of the Church as they seek God's will in whatever situation they may find themselves. We must expect occasionally to be warned or corrected: 'Those whom I love, I reprove and chasten,' the Lord told the church in Laodicea, though few exercising a gift of simple prophecy today will want to speak to their fellow Christians as fiercely as the prophetic author of the Book of Revelation (3:19)! God's aim in prophecy is to encourage us, not to discourage us. The Holy Spirit will warn us of the dangers of disobedience and fear within our own inspired thoughts rather than through the inspired words of another Christian. Prophecy given in love does not bludgeon us into repentance; it prepares us for moving into that contrition for sin which places us under the cross of Jesus Christ.

We must distinguish between the gift of prophecy and the gift of teaching if we are to appreciate the purpose of the former charism in the Church's life. In the Old Testament the teacher stood in the tradition of the law. It was his task to meditate upon the law and 'to seek and to search out by wisdom all that is done under heaven' (Eccles. 1:13). His spiritual gift was to be able to assimilate all that he had learned and to instruct and enlighten the people expounding known truths with a mind inspired by God to convey teaching to his listeners. The prophet spoke more from the impulse of a sudden revelation and his utterances were more likely to be exhortations to awaken the feelings and the consciences of his hearers. So in the Church today it is the gift of teaching which is manifested in the pulpit and lecture room rather than the gift of prophecy, though occasionally a sermon will be led by the Holy Spirit into prophetic paths.

The gift of prophecy can enable worshippers to sing spontaneously in worship. David set apart 'certain of the sons of Asaph, and of Heman, and of Jeduthun, who should prophesy with lyres, with harps, and with cymbals' (1 Chron. 25:1), and when Paul distinguished 'spiritual songs' from 'psalms and hymns' (Col. 3:16), he may well have been thinking of acts of praise sung by inspiration in worship. I once heard a girl sing a beautiful hymn to the risen Christ as an impromptu solo during a eucharist. I did not know the hymn, and no one else joined in, so I concluded that it was a new composition.

But when I asked her after the service where it came from, she said hesitantly that God gave it to her at that moment and that she could not remember much about the words or the melody.

Prayers uttered in the spirit of prophecy have a unique beauty. They are as fresh as a cool breeze in an act of worship that is stuffy and stale. Sometimes they echo orations of long ago, testifying to the timelessness of the Spirit who inspires them. Since reading about the Jewish *berakah* (prayers of blessing) and their relationship to the early eucharistic prayers of the Church, I have been struck how often extemporary prayers, spoken in a prophetic manner through people who knew nothing of liturgical forms, have followed the spirit and shape of Jewish benedictions.

(iii)

Members of charismatic groups find prophecies given in pictures which come vividly into the mind of one or more members. One member will say, 'The Lord has given me a picture,' and then he will go on to describe it. Sometimes another will say that he can see it too. Others may ask questions on points of detail about the picture.

Like the interpretations and prophecies, these pictures also created difficulties for me. How could one be sure that they were not pictures of the imagination, perhaps surfacing from the unconscious after years of lying dormant there? And why should God choose this roundabout way of communicating with his people? Yet I knew visionary experiences of different kinds, from the great sheet full of animals, reptiles and birds that Peter had on the housetop at Joppa, to the extended series of revelations given to the author of the Book of Revelation, are an integral part of God's revelation of his will to his people, and they have been given to all kinds of Christians throughout the centuries as God guided and encouraged his servants. Less is said about them nowadays in Church circles because we do not want to appear to be attributing mystical powers to ourselves.

So I slowly learned to be more open to the possibility that God might communicate with his people in this way, and I realized that some of the things which were taught through the pictures which my friends described during prayer were lessons which were best taught in a pictorial form.

After we had been at Whatcombe for some months and had encountered the stresses and strains of community living, I was in a prayer group with the other members of the community when I saw in my mind's eye what looked like several pieces of a jigsaw puzzle converging towards one another. Then I recognized that the 'pieces' were cut into the shape of human forms. For a moment they came neatly together. But because they were living pieces they were changing their shape constantly and their unity was broken by their individual movements so that the process of fitting them together had to begin all over again. Although the picture did not mean anything to me, I felt I ought to describe it to the group. When I had done this someone said they saw it as a pattern of community living. God works in us individually as well as in community; and as we are changing under his grace in different ways, we are constantly having to rediscover our unity with each other in him. The picture was so vivid that we often recalled it when relationships within the community became strained. Encouraged by the realization that stresses were often caused by the process of growing together, we were able to discuss and pray through our problems until a richer unity emerged.

At a charismatic meeting in Belfast I heard a young Jesuit seminarian describe a picture he had received during prayer before he left Dublin the previous day. He had never travelled north of the border into Ulster before in his life, and he had been worried about the reception he might receive from what he knew would be a Protestant audience in a troubled city. He had been interested in ecumenism, but only in a detached way. In his prayer he saw a picture hanging on the wall in an elaborate frame. Although the painting was all white, it was a beautiful picture in that setting, and he felt himself admiring it. Then the white colouring inside the frame changed until a pattern of reds, greens, blues, yellows, oranges and other colours covered the surface, and he knew that it was a more beautiful picture than before. 'God showed me that his Church was made up of different kinds of Christians, not just Roman Catholics,' he explained, 'and I knew from that moment that he would give me a love for Protestants in Northern Ireland that I had never had before.' The warm response of that audience can be imagined: they had learned more about unity in diversity through his picture than they would have done in a series of lectures on ecumenism.

CHAPTER VI

DO ALL POSSESS GIFTS OF HEALING?

(i)

CHARISMS of tongues, interpretation and prophecy rest upon faith in the operation of the Holy Spirit within ourselves— faith that he will take the sounds that we utter and mould them into prayer for his glory, faith that he will inspire us to say aloud what he wishes to communicate at that particular moment. Most Christians seem to face a 'sound barrier' which prevents them speaking their faith in various ways—talking to others about their beliefs, using the name 'Jesus' in conversation, saying a prayer aloud with others, as well as accepting the gifts of the Spirit which we have been discussing. Not one of the least important ways in which we are edified—built up in the faith—is in the breaking of this sound barrier when we begin to speak in tongues, to interpret and to prophecy. As our faith grows through these charisms, we are led to offer ourselves for other forms of ministry for which the Holy Spirit brings the appropriate grace.

One such ministry is healing. In these days the Church is recovering her confidence that she has been given this ministry. Prayers for and with the sick, the laying on of hands and unction, and healing services are becoming common. Yet there are still many Christians who do not regard this ministry as one in which they all share because they are baptized with water and the Holy Spirit. It is still 'special'—the concern of the clergy, hospital chaplains, and a few 'gifted' lay people.

Reserve of this kind has its value. It means that most Christians will approach the ministry with care and sensitivity. But this reserve can also weaken the Church's proclamation of the Gospel, for the New Testament shows that the healing of the sick was one of the signs that followed that proclamation. More than one source behind the narratives of the evangelists contains the tradition that Christ commissioned his disciples to 'heal the sick, raise the dead, cleanse lepers, cast out demons' (Mt. 10: 8; Lk. 9: 2; 10: 9), when he sent them out to preach the kingdom of God. How much more powerful the Church's witness to the authenticity of the Gospel would be if healing was seen to be done through her fellowship in the Spirit!

Confusion is caused by a failure to recognize the difference between gifts of healing and the ministry of the healer. Certain individuals are called by God to exercise the ministry of a healer within the Church. With them the charism is a more or less continuous grace operating through their lives as they are obedient to God. Some, like the late Dorothy Kerin of Burrswood, have been commissioned to this ministry by the Church.

Gifts of healing (the plural, *charismata iamatōn*, should be noted) refers to those charisms which are given to a Christian in a particular situation. There is no reason to suppose that these are limited to a few members of the Body of Christ. God may use any of us to aid the healing of another as we commit ourselves in faith to him. It may only be grace to listen with loving concern to someone else's troubles for half-an-hour or to say a prayer with a friend in hospital; but it can be a gift of healing that startles us by its effect, once we are willing to embark on this ministry in faith.

The place to begin is in the home and among one's friends. A parishioner in Romford sat by the bedside of her sick, four-year-old son at night, wondering what would quieten him after a restless hour. Suddenly she felt prompted to lay a hand on his head and pray aloud for him. Within minutes he was peacefully asleep. Months later, the roles were reversed. One hot afternoon the mother lay on the bed with a fierce headache and told her son not to bother her. He came to the bedside, placed his hand on her forehead, said, 'Jesus, please make Mummy better,' and soon her headache had gone.

The gifts of the Holy Spirit are wonderfully adapted to

59

our capacities. God does not ask us to exercise a ministry which is far beyond the reach of our imaginations—at any rate, not without a gift of faith to enable us to accept it! He leads us step by step. A churchman who has not exercised gifts of healing is not likely to be called by God to lay hands on the patient with limbs smashed in a car accident or with a terminal illness! There is an apprenticeship in little things first. To start with he will be led to pray with those afflicted with headaches, colds, insomnia, and so on. Gradually, when he sees God healing minor ailments through his ministry, he will be guided to more serious illnesses. Willingness to be used in faith will show him if his ministry has a permanent quality—whether or not people are regularly healed after he has prayed with them. If so, then he should thank God for the gracious gift and pray for guidance and discernment in exercising it.

(ii)

Here are a few practical suggestions of the way to minister gifts of healing in simple, domestic situations involving minor ailments.

Commit the opportunity in a short silent prayer to God and suggest to the sufferer that you pray with him aloud. Begin by asking the Lord to accept yours and the sufferer's penitence for any sins that may separate you both from him. Then continue by claiming healing for the sufferer in the name of Jesus Christ in a direct way, for example,

'Father in heaven,
  your Son, Jesus Christ, called us
  to preach the Gospel and to heal the sick,
  and promised that whatever we asked in his Name,
  we would receive:
  heal this affliction,
  pour the balm of your restoring Spirit
  into every part of——'s body
  that he may be completely cured
  to your glory.'

60

If the nature of the ailment causes pain or discomfort it is helpful to specify the nerves, muscles, and fibres involved, pausing and invoking God's healing for each one.

The prayer should be said slowly and authoritatively. There is no place in such a petition for the qualifying phrase, 'If it be God's will.' 'The prayer of faith will save the sick man, and the Lord will raise him up,' says the epistle of James (5:15). It is God's business, not ours, if the prayer does not appear to be answered. We should only qualify our prayer when the Holy Spirit prompts us to pray in a conditional manner.

Usually we shall want to touch the invalid as we are praying for him. The laying on of hands is the traditional means by which the one who ministers associates himself with the one to whom he is ministering. If possible, stand slightly to one side of the patient. Place one hand across the forehead so that the little finger rests just above the eyebrows; place the other hand behind the head so that the head is held rather as one would hold a football. The clasp should be gentle but firm: this gives the patient the sensation of being sympathetically supported. Hands should not be placed on top of the head for a long period as they can soon feel heavy and oppressive.

After finishing the prayer, suggest to the invalid that he thanks God for the promised healing and accepts it in faith. Vocalizing his response in this way helps to build up faith and to co-operate with the healing work of the Spirit. To thank God even before there are signs of healing is a powerful expression of trust in him, demonstrating that we stand on 'the assurance of things hoped for, the conviction of things not seen.'

Ministry of this kind does not, of course, mean neglecting other services of a practical nature to a sick person—visiting them, making them comfortable, offering to fetch the prescription, and so on. The parish priest or minister should be informed of what has happened. And ministry of this kind certainly does not mean that we are attempting to bypass all that is done by doctors, nurses and others for the relief of suffering. Christians should be the first to recognize that many charisms of healing are given through the medical profession, even through those who do not claim Jesus as Lord. The person who is sick but who refuses to go to the doctor because he says 'Jesus will heal', is probably trying to spiritualize an unadmitted fear of diagnosis and treatment. But, at the same time, Christians have a ministry of prayer and charism in the whole work of healing and we should be prepared to exercise it.

I have rarely prayed for and laid hands on a patient without tingling doubts in my mind. Will it be 'successful'? What will the patient think if nothing happens? I recognize that such doubts arise from the wrong idea that in some way the ministry is mine, not God's. But still the doubts come—though I have noticed that when I am most dubious the healing is sometimes most striking!

A young couple arrived at Whatcombe for a conference, bringing a baby with them aged a few months. They laid his carrycot on the floor and pulled back his clothes to show me his skin reddened with eczema. He had been like this for two or three weeks, they said. Would I pray for him? Without any preliminaries I bent over the cot, said a short prayer, and made the sign of the cross over the baby. I soon forgot the incident; but three days later in the conference, when the mother pulled back his clothes again to show me, the baby's skin was perfectly clear.

During the period when we were engaged in the massive do-it-ourselves operation to get Whatcombe ready as a conference centre, Jean began to feel sharp pains in her arms. The pains kept her awake at night and they became a burden to her. One Sunday evening, while the community was assembled for prayers, she asked me to lay hands on her for healing. She was sitting in a chair with her arms lifted upwards in the *orans* position, so as I prayed, I was prompted to touch her bare arms and bring her hands together as I said the final 'Amen.' She said afterwards that she felt the pain leave her arms as my hands moved over them.

At a eucharist celebrated during a conference on the

ministry of healing, I was asked to lay hands on a member for healing. After everyone had received communion, I made the woman sit in a chair in the centre of the chapel and I invited the thirty or so other members of the conference to minister the laying on of hands with me, either by touching the woman lightly themselves or by stretching their hands out towards her (as the clergy do when a bishop ordains a priest). The sense of joint ministry to that person was powerful in that chapel that morning. And as I stood there with the members of the conference surrounding me, I realized more clearly than ever before how all our ministries in the Spirit, as clergy as well as laity, are ministries of the Church. 'Body ministry' is the phrase used in charismatic circles to express this—it is not as individuals that God works through us but as what we are in the Body of Christ.

I once addressed a junior clergy conference on the subject of healing. When I had finished, one of the members said: 'Canon —— was organizing this conference, but he couldn't come because he's slipped and sprained his back. Why don't you call on him and pray for him?'

Excuses leapt into my mind, but they hardly seemed plausible in view of what I had said!

Then the Lord gave me an idea.

'It'll take about half-an-hour to reach him from here by car,' I said. 'If you men will pray together for fifteen minutes at about the time I get to his house, I'll go and visit him.'

They agreed.

Thirty minutes later I was entering the sick man's room. He was sitting in a chair by his bed, his face white with pain. I did not know him very well, and I wondered how he would react to the young clergyman's suggestion.

To my relief, he seemed pleased when I explained the purpose of my visit, and began to look a little better.

'When you've prayed for me, I'll pray for them,' he said; and we spent a short time in prayer together, during which I asked God to heal his back.

When we'd finished, he grasped the arms of his chair.

'Now I'd better try,' he said.

I felt humbled. This man had greater faith than I had!

He stood up, slowly stretched up to his full height, and took several steps across the room and back again.

'I haven't been able to do that before!' he commented, as he sat down again. 'It certainly seems easier.'

(iii)

Though they may show themselves in physical ways, many sicknesses are psychological and spiritual, and opportunities for the Christian to exercise gifts of healing through prayerful and sympathetic listening are boundless. Training in counselling techniques is useful as a preparation for this ministry, but the Christian can never be purely clinical in his approach. He is to show the compassion of Jesus Christ towards the one with a problem, and it is the Holy Spirit who gives this compassion, a colour in the rainbow of divine love that shines through the Body of Christ.

Along with the training and practice in counselling, we learn to rely also on 'the utterance of knowledge according to the same Spirit' (1 Cor. 12:8). This charism enables us to see beyond what is presented to us as we listen to what is troubling the person deep down. An analyst learns to do this through years of counselling. A Christian who is sensitive to what the Spirit says to him in other ministries finds that, as he talks to someone with a problem, he will be given questions or comments to put to his companion which enable him to understand the problem more clearly.

The memory is stirred, a forgotten pain is uncovered, and the source of a problem is tracked down back in the person's history, perhaps to the influence of a parent or the shock of an unpleasant experience in early life. Involvement in spiritualism, the occult and black magic bring their own tragedies. The spiritual gift of knowledge is precious in this searching and supportive ministry in the name of Jesus Christ.

After listening and counselling, I usually end with a prayer —and sometimes the laying on of hands—asking God to heal the hurts that have been forgotten but not forgiven, the broken relationships that have left their debris for years spoiling a life. I take each point that my companion has made and use it as the subject of prayer—confession, petition, thanksgiving—and then, as with physical healing, I encourage him or her to claim the healing power of the Holy Spirit through faith in Jesus Christ. Sometimes it is a costly ministry for the two involved: 'If one member suffers, all suffer together' (1 Cor. 12:26). But it is rewarding as one sees God at work in people, changing and renewing them. In no other way is the truth of Paul's saying more evident than in those freed from their past: 'We are not children of the slave but of the free woman' (Gal. 4:31).

To exercise gifts of healing is to manifest the charismatic nature of the Church and the authority of Christ which has been committed to us. 'These signs will accompany those who believe' are words belonging to a later, editorial addition to St. Mark (16:17), but this should not obscure the truth they contain. The 'signs' are not only the sacraments; they are also ministries in the Spirit. It may be that the Christian who exercises gifts of healing in the name of Jesus does not witness an unbroken series of 'successes' as a result of it. I have never seen a miraculous, instantaneous healing of the sort recorded in the gospels (though I hope to one day). I have prayed for some sick people without any apparent physical benefit. And I have also prayed for a few to be healed and seen them die—including a tragic case involving a little boy aged seven. The more we are used in the ministry of healing, the more we enter into the mystery of Jesus Christ's own ministry, with his suffering and cry of dereliction from the cross as well as with his resurrection and his reassuring words, 'It is I myself' (Luke 24:39). We cannot know how that mystery will work out in the life of the sick man or woman. But I have also seen people healed remarkably swiftly after ministering to them in the way I have described. We act in faith—the work is God's.

65

E

CHAPTER VII

SPIRITUAL HOSTS

(i)

WHEN in the early 'sixties the Church of England debated whether or not to remove references to the devil from the *Revised Catechism*, I was not unduly worried. I thought vaguely at the time that if the references were removed, it might make it easier to use the catechism with the sceptical teenagers I taught in confirmation classes, but otherwise the debate did not interest me. I was prepared to discount much that is written in the New Testament about the devil and demon possession as relics of first century attitudes. The Gadarene swine stampeded down the slope of the hill into the lake because they were frightened by the noise the possessed man was making among the tombs; Jesus 'rebuked' the fever that afflicted Simon's mother-in-law because for him the fever was a manifestation of an evil spirit. I was confident that medical and psychological studies could explain much that was attributed to the devil and his minions in the apostolic age.

But since I have become more aware of the Holy Spirit's activity in the world, in the Church and in the individual, I have also become more aware of the darker spiritual realms. This is, I have discovered, a common experience among those who have received the baptism with the Spirit. We become more conscious that the forces which destroy people, and which destroy relationships between people, are often apart from themselves although at work in them. It is no longer satisfying to argue that a man is what he is only because of the circumstances of his birth, his upbringing, his career, his wife and children, and the observable pressures that influence him. We have to take into account those spiritual pressures which the author of Ephesians referred to when he wrote, 'We are not contending against flesh and blood, but against principalities, against the powers, against the world rulers of this present darkness, against the spiritual hosts of wickedness in the heavenly places' (Eph. 6: 12). It is only when we begin to minister to certain people on the supposition that they are under the power of the devil that they are released from fears and tensions which have built up within them.

A young woman came into a prayer group one day looking ill. Although she was on the best of terms with all the members, she had found it increasingly difficult to pray with them during the few weeks in which she had been a member of the group. She kept silent during the Bible reading and the discussion that followed it, but when the prayers began the tensions within her suddenly sharpened. She noticed that they seemed stretched to breaking-point when the name 'Jesus' was mentioned. Then, when someone began speaking in a tongue, she writhed and screamed in a voice that was unrecognizable as belonging to her. Two or three of us stood round her, laid hands on her head and shoulders, and prayed. Someone invoked the power of the cross of Christ over evil and commanded the devil to come out of her and to go to the place God had prepared for him. We summoned the Holy Spirit to fill her afresh, and I traced the sign of the cross on her forehead. Immediately she calmed down, and within a few minutes was her normal self.

Later she was able to describe the experience. A terrifying force had taken hold of her body, she said, and she had been unable to control the rising fears and tensions. Intellectually she had felt detached from those fears and tensions, but they had so overwhelmed her that she had been unable to prevent herself writhing and screaming. The horror of the experience arose not only from fear of this mysterious force but also from the knowledge that her response to it was beyond her control. We discovered later that years previously she had been involved in spiritualism and that there was a history of this involvement in her family. The ministry given to her by the group marked a moment of renewal in her life, and from

67

that time she grew stronger in resisting the assaults of this strange force.

It would have been more in harmony with modern attitudes if the group had told her to calm down and then tried to reason with her why she had reacted in this way. They might have suggested that there was in her an unconscious reaction against the supernatural, originating perhaps in rejections she had experienced in childhood or youth. Or they might have suggested that she was reacting against something that transferred itself to religious symbols like the name of our Lord and the sound of speaking in tongues. But because the group chose to act on the un-modern assumption that what the New Testament says about devil possession and the victory of Christ over evil was true, the young woman was brought to an assurance in the power of God in her life.

I have called their attitude 'un-modern', yet this is a misnomer. Modern technological man is increasingly fascinated by the supernatural. Evidence grows each year that in Britain and elsewhere more and more people are dabbling in spiritualism, the occult, divination, fortune-telling and weird cults brought in by *gurus* from the East. Even intelligent people seem to be involved, first out of mild curiosity, then with a deepening interest as the 'hobby' tightens its grip on them. Some of the leaders and enthusiasts of these practices are earnest, well-meaning men and women; but sincerity is no protection against Satan. 'There is a way which seems right to a man, but its end is the way of death' (Prov. 14: 12). The young person who plays with a ouija-board for half-an-hour's entertainment is exposing himself to an evil influence of which he can have no possible conception; the housewife who consults the oracles printed in her women's weekly magazine could be falling into the insiduous grasp of an enemy who is using the amiable, educated contributor of that weekly item for his own purposes.

'When he (the Holy Spirit) comes, he will convince the world of sin and of righteousness and of judgment: of sin, because they do not believe in me; of righteousness, because I go to the Father, and you will see me no more; of judgment, because the ruler of this world is judged' (Jn. 16: 8–11). Behind this saying in the Johannine discourse lies the truth that as the Holy Spirit enlightens the Christian, he is able to discern more clearly the impulses and motives that lie behind his own and other people's conduct. The Spirit exposes our own sin, clearing the way for the gift of repentance; and he also exposes the work of the devil behind conduct and practices in others which from a human point of view may appear harmless and indeed beneficial. This is the only way I can account for the suspicion and then revulsion that has grown in me over the past few years for these kind of things which people are being involved in and which I formerly regarded with a tolerant amusement.

(ii)

Both the Old and the New Testaments condemn without reservation all attempts to pierce the veil between this world and the realm of the spirit, either by trying to communicate with the dead, or to foretell the future, or to enter into communion with powers other than the power of God himself. When Elymas the magician sought to turn Sergius Paulus, the proconsul, away from the Christian faith, 'Paul, filled with the Holy Spirit, looked intently at him and said, "You son of the devil, you enemy of all righteousness, full of all deceit and vanity, will you not stop making crooked the straight paths of the Lord?" ' (Acts 13: 9). Behind this outright condemnation is the implication that those who seek to pierce the veil lack faith in God, that they do not believe God has already provided adequate channels and means for hearing his voice and knowing his will. Our God is the Lord of all—the dead as well as the living, the future as well as the past and the present, the invisible as well as the visible. 'And when they say to you, "Consult the mediums and the wizards who chirp and mutter", should not a people consult their God? Should they consult the dead on behalf of the living?' (Isa. 8: 19).

Shortly after I went to Romford, I officiated at the funeral of a man of about sixty and a few days later called on the widow to see how she was. In the course of the conversation the topic of survival after death came up, and I attempted to lead her to faith in God for her husband's salvation. I saw a little of her after that but gradually forgot about her as other matters occupied my attention. Months later I heard she had committed suicide. A neighbour told me that after her husband's death she had begun to attend spiritualist seances and had received 'messages.' At the time I concluded that the suicide had been caused by excessive grief and guilt-feelings. Now, looking back after several years' experience of how the devil can influence people through spiritualism, I lean towards a different conclusion.

Yet it is easy to slip into the trap of attributing every misfortune immediately to Satan without looking first for more natural causes. We need to seek the charism of discerning of spirits and at the same time not to pretend that we have this gift when we have no definite guidance in talking to someone who has a problem they wish to share with us. As a general rule, it is safest to assume that a problem has its origins in the physical or psychological causes unless another cause is revealed. Let the devil reveal himself. Don't go looking for him!

A man in his mid-twenties asked me to talk to him during a weekend conference at Whatcombe and we had a long session together during which he told me something of his past life. The son of a broken home, he had struggled through school and college in spite of a rebellious and immoral life, which included drug-taking. When he was about twenty he had been converted to faith in Jesus Christ and had tried to live as a faithful Christian ever since.

'I don't fall to temptations as I used to,' he said, 'and I know God has forgiven me for all that I did in the past, but I still don't feel right. It is as if a thick, oily substance is clinging round my soul, holding me back from being truly free in the Spirit.'

Up to this point, I had regarded our interview as a simple counselling session of a supportive kind, to end perhaps with a prayer committing the situation to God. But the reference to 'a thick, oily substance', puzzled me. What did this mean? We talked about it for a time, and then I asked: 'Do you think there is anything I can do about it?'

'Yes,' he said. 'I'd be grateful if you'd ask God to take this oily stuff away.'

Still puzzled, I closed my eyes. I said a straightforward general intercession for cleansing and peace and then I stopped, wondering what to say next. At that moment, I had a clear direction from God to go and lay my hands on the man. As I did so, I began to speak in tongues quietly.

The effect was dramatic. Immediately the young man began to shake, his face was flushed and puffed, his arms and legs shot out in a wild fashion and he made dreadful grunting noises. Holding his head, I felt as if I was struggling with an animal.

It was not until this moment that I had the slightest suspicion that I was dealing with a case of evil possession. I continued to pray in tongues, louder now. Should I command the devil to depart from him in the name of Christ? I wondered. Then I remembered that earlier in the week I had read the texts of exorcisms pronounced over catechumens at the scrutinies which were organized in the early Church prior to their baptisms. I spoke one aloud with an authority that was not mine, using words like these:

'I exorcize you, evil spirit, in the name of the Father and of the Son and of the Holy Spirit, that you may leave this servant of God alone and, as Christ himself commanded you, to get behind him and go away. Amen.'

The struggling ceased, and in a few moments I was able to leave the young man and sit down. I prayed that the Holy Spirit might fill him with peace and strength and protect him from further assaults by the enemy. Then I opened my eyes.

He was staring at me with a look of astonished happiness on his face.

'What happened?' I asked.

Slowly and deliberately he replied, "A flame of fire came down from heaven and burned up all that thick, oily stuff. . . . I'm fine! I'm free!'

And he cried for joy.

The following day, Sunday, at the morning eucharist, as we were exchanging the peace among ourselves in the congregation, he came over to me and gave me an exuberant hug.

'I never believed the Lord could bless me so much in one weekend,' he said.

I saw a friend of his about a year later. I learned that he was a changed man—full of joy in the Spirit and powerful in his witness to Jesus Christ.

(iii)

'The reason the Son of God appeared was to destroy the works of the devil' (1 Jn. 3:8). A Christian who is faithful cannot be possessed by the devil, but he can be tempted and influenced through the weaker points in his personality. It requires both a knowledge of psychology and a charism of discernment to detect when a person is being attacked in the unconscious depths of his being. The well-meaning counsellor with limited experience can do damage through insensitivity. Anyone whose problem seems more complex than appeared initially, or who does not respond to a straightforward ministry of listening and prayer, should be referred to a qualified Christian priest or psychiatrist.

The report of the commission convened by the Bishop of Exeter on exorcism has wise advice on this.[1] The report's weakness is that it assumes such a ministry can only be undertaken by an ordained priest who may not act without the explicit permission of the diocesan bishop, as laid down in Canon LXXII of 1604, but since it was written for the Church of England it is understandable that the commission had to make its recommendations within the structure of Anglican discipline. Behind the ruling of the canon is the knowledge that those who embark on this ministry are exposing themselves to spiritual dangers of which the uninformed priest or layman can hardly imagine, and this warning must always be heeded. The report lays down a sensible pattern for the preparation of the ministers and the patient, the pro-

72

cedure to be adopted for the ministry, and the aftercare of those assisted in this way. The advice that ministers should act in pairs, and that when the patient is a woman another woman should be present, is supported by common experience in this ministry in charismatic circles today.

Can the devil's influence overshadow places? Can he misdirect the physical movement of natural and manufactured objects? The two leaders of a house group I know often pray before the members arrive that the room the group meets in will be protected by God from the enemy. They say the prayer seems to make the meetings happier and more fruitful. When we arrived at Whatcombe we sensed an evil presence in certain rooms which disappeared after we had gone round the house praying that God would make each one his dwelling-place.

One dark January evening, during a clergy conference at Whatcombe, a speaker said in a discussion that he believed that the devil sometimes used motor car accidents to kill or injure Christians. This, he said, seemed to him to be the only explanation for certain kinds of accidents that Christian people he knew had been involved in.

Had I been present at that conference, I would probably have raised a large question-mark in my mind over that discussion. Could the devil nudge the elbow of a driver or cause the brakes to fail? I might have asked. But at that moment—about 5.30 p.m.—I was driving across the New Forest in the midst of two long streams of home-going traffic. Ahead of me and behind me a line of vehicles moved with dipped headlights at about thirty-five miles an hour in a westward direction. To my right the east-bound stream of traffic flashed past, the headlights coming into my view and swishing past at intervals of three or four seconds.

Suddenly, one pair of headlights from the on-coming traffic swerved out of the stream and leapt straight at me. I swung my Morris Minor onto the grass verge to my left. The car scraped the side of my vehicle and rammed the van that was following me in a headlong collision.

The car and the van were total wrecks, but fortunately no

one was seriously injured. The driver of the offending car, travelling home from work with three passengers, had no idea what had caused him to steer his car across double-white lines and attempt to overtake in impossibly dangerous conditions. And I, as I slowly drove my damaged Morris back to What-combe, wondered why out of all those hundreds of cars on the New Forest road that evening, it should have been mine that had been placed in a position of extreme jeopardy.

Then, when I got back to Whatcombe and learned what the conference had been discussing, I realized with an odd sensation that accident had happened almost at the same moment as that the speaker had been making his debatable suggestion. . . .

(iv)

If an encounter with the Holy Spirit enables us to discern more clearly than before the work of the devil, we need wisdom not to attribute to him everything unfortunate or un-pleasant that happens to us. There is an unhealthy tendency in some quarters to 'give place to the devil' in quite unneces-sary ways. Some people blame the devil if they miss the train —whereas in fact they should have got up earlier and kept an eye on the clock. They go to bed too late, get up feeling out of sorts, the milk boils over, the children are difficult, the boss throws his weight around—but the truth is that they are not being attacked by the devil: they lack 'a sound mind' and 'the peace of God.'

We are still liable, after we have been baptized in the Spirit, to walk not according to the Spirit but according to the flesh, and it is the old carnal, self-life that is responsible for difficulties such as these. It is normal for 'the old man' to be fearful, fretful, irritable and full of tension, with a tendency to sensuality thrown in. What we need when we are in such a state is not an exorcism but the power of the cross of Christ, to crucify the flesh with its passions and desires.

So a Christian who has made it a discipline to confess his sins before a priest from time to time does not abandon the practice when he is baptized with the Holy Spirit. On the contrary, he finds that the Spirit leads him to a fuller repentance than he has known before. Peter's sermon on the day of Pentecost ended with a call to repent; and although that call was to men and women who were outside the fellowship of the newly-born Church, yet it is applicable to each of us while we are in danger of falling into the temptations presented by the world, the flesh and the devil. We daily sin against God and need constant and repeated forgiveness. And we daily sin against our fellow men. It is from this acknowledgment of our failings and our brokenness that God takes us and recreates us as a new person in him. It is in repentance—to echo John the Baptist's proclamation—that the kingdom of heaven is at hand for each of us.[2]

The priest who hears confessions has an opportunity, not only to pronounce the absolution, but also to minister in the Spirit to the penitent in the ways discussed in this book. The formal counsel in the confessional may be extended in an interview elsewhere. Prayers of healing, deliverance and strengthening may be necessary. Some penitents have received the Spirit more fully into their lives after making their confession aided by the ministry of their confessor. We need to recover a concept of the sacrament of penance which goes beyond an idea that we must 'get rid of our sins' to one that includes reconciliation with God and with our fellow men and renewal in the Spirit.[3]

But in whatever shape the temptation comes, we know that through the indwelling of the Holy Spirit we are caught up into the life of God in such a way that only our wilful unrepentance can break the bond of love. The world, the flesh and the devil have no power over us. We may feel their effects, but they are not invincible. 'And after you have suffered a little while, the God of all grace, who has called you to his eternal glory in Christ, will himself restore, establish, and strengthen you' (1 Pet. 5:10).

75

NOTES

1 *Exorcism: the findings of a Commission convened by the Bishop of Exeter,* ed. Robert Petitpierre, O.S.B., S.P.C.K., 1972.
2 Basilea Schlink, *Repentance: the Joy-filled Life,* Oliphants, 1969, pp. 13 ff.
3 Michael Scanlan, T.O.R.., *The Power in Penance,* Ave Maria Press, Notre Dame, Indiana, 1972.

CHAPTER VIII

FELLOWSHIP IN THE SPIRIT

(i)

'YOU cannot know for sure where the Holy Spirit is going to act and bring renewal. You really can't. The Spirit still, like the wind, blows where he wishes. And without issuing weather forecasts! Only one sign appears often enough to betray his intentions. In the history of renewal, revivals, holiness movements, in church life, the period immediately before some fresh outpouring of the Spirit seems to be marked by a burden for prayer in the hearts of at least a small core of Christians in an area. I have been impressed recently, in different parts of the country, to find groups meeting in just this sort of way. Expectantly, open to God for whatever he may have for them, for their town, for their congregations. I wonder sometimes whether this may not prove to be the most significant of all the facts in the scene we have been surveying.'[1]

So wrote John Poulton, the Research and Development Officer of the Archbishops' Council on Evangelism, in a recent book on evangelism today. Among the groups he met were those who had been brought together as a result of their members' baptism with the Holy Spirit.

Since it is the work of the Spirit to draw Christians together into the Body of Christ, those who receive him more fully into their lives feel the need for closer relationships with other Christians. They look round the members of the congregation in their local church on Sundays and wish that there could be a deeper sharing in the things of God. Not that they want to abandon formal worship—far from it. But they long for opportunities for seeking God's will more intimately, for personal praying, for telling and hearing of the joys and problems of Christian discipleship. In short, they want to be together more.

'All together in one place'—it is striking the way the New Testament refers so often to the corporate nature of the Church. This reference peeps through, not only in the theologican expositions of the Church as the Body of Christ and the Vine, but also in incidental ways. The word *allelōn*, 'one another,' rings like a bell through its pages—'accept one another,' 'serve one another,' 'wash one another's feet,' 'confess your sins to one another and pray one for another,' 'forbearing one another and forgiving each other,' 'teaching and admonishing one another,' 'comfort one another and build each other up,' 'bear one another's burdens,' 'love one another as I have loved you.'[2]

Evidence of being baptized with the Spirit is not the use of spiritual gifts. To speak with tongues and yet to use our tongues to be critical of others is to deny the love of God which should be manifested by the Holy Spirit through us. 'If I speak in the tongues of men and of angels, but have not love, I am a noisy gong or a clanging cymbal' (1 Cor. 13:1). In chapter thirteen of 1 Corinthians the apostle listed again the charisms he had catalogued in chapter twelve and affirmed that without love they made him as nothing. The real evidence of the divine indwelling, he said elsewhere, is the fruit of the Spirit: love, joy, peace, patience, kindness, goodness, faithfulness, gentleness, self-control (Gal. 5:22). But these are virtues in human relationships; they are fruits that together produce the harvest of Christian unity. For all that we have said so far about spiritual gifts, the greatest charism of all is the love which God gives to make his people one with him and with each other. 'By one Spirit we were all baptized into one body' (1 Cor. 12:13) communicants of the Church of England hear before they give one another the sign of mutual love, the peace, in their new eucharistic liturgies. The Holy Spirit draws us together.

So when Christians are baptized with the Holy Spirit the result is a prayer meeting. The first few people in a congregation to receive the pentecostal experience begin to meet in one another's homes. Others join them. Then further developments take place. Either the group increases until it becomes necessary to use a larger hall for the gathering (a charismatic group in Dublin, beginning in 1972 with twelve members in the lounge of Kimmage Manor, the home of the Holy Ghost Fathers, expanded to five hundred within a year and had to move to various larger meeting-places). Or the group subdivides and spawns other groups.

Often both evolve simultaneously. The larger meeting is held on a midweek evening in the church hall and given a title. A Birmingham parish calls it 'Open to God,' a Baptist church in London 'Fellowship Evening.' Participants sit in rows or in a wide circle singing hymns and choruses, listening to Bible readings and talks, and joining in free prayer during which there may be speaking in tongues, interpretations and prophecies. Those requiring healing are prayed for and have hands laid on them by the leader or by those called to that ministry. The counselling of individuals takes place during or after the meeting. Visitors are introduced with news of what God is doing elsewhere. The atmosphere is relaxed and happy.

The singing of choruses is a characteristic of these meetings. Some choruses are new, inspired by the renewal movement; others are traditional, originating in revival campaigns of former years. They proclaim Gospel truths in a simple way, mingled with an appeal for and assurances of divine aid. Prominent themes are affirmations of devotion to the Person of Jesus Christ and of love among fellow-Christians. Staid church-goers are sometimes puzzled when they first encounter choruses at charismatic assemblies. They have not previously associated this sort of singing with Christian worship! Yet when sensitively chosen and led, choruses do much to create an atmosphere of corporate devotion and they provide a wealth of material through which worshippers may express their response to God. Since many choruses are easily memorized, they can be used spontaneously during prayer and praise: one person begins singing a chorus at an inspired moment, the rest taking it up in a wave of corporate devotion. Guitars, tambourines, castanets and a piano—the range of accompaniment is wide. The one instrument that these meetings seem to avoid is the church organ!

But the smaller prayer group—numbering anything up to twenty—is of fundamental importance. In fact, it is essential for anyone baptized with the Spirit. Without it their spiritual growth is stunted. I have already explained that for three years after my pentecostal experience I felt the lack of a prayer fellowship. At Whatcombe we always take particular care, when an individual is baptized with the Spirit, to link him or her up with a group.

(ii)

In the prayer meeting the scriptures open themselves up for us in their amazing richness. We meet another charism—'the utterance of wisdom' (1 Cor. 12: 8), when a flash of inspiration, given to us or to another, reveals the wisdom in God's Word in a new and relevant way. We may have used Bible reading notes and commentaries, and we may have studied the scriptures at school and in college in preparation for examinations; but nothing feeds us so satisfyingly with the Bread of the Word than the reverent reading of a passage of scripture in a group, the silent waiting on the Holy Spirit, and the exchange of thoughts that spring out of the text. Discussions and disagreements there may be, but as long as those who are assembled remain aware of the Holy Spirit's presence, the group can contain these within its bond of love. We know that he who sent the Spirit promised that the Counsellor would lead us into all truth. Discussions and disagreements are signs that members of the group are still struggling to receive the truth which is in Jesus Christ, the fulness of which is anyway beyond their comprehension.

From corporate meditation on scripture the group moves into prayer. Usually it is extemporary prayer, though formal material—a collect, a psalm, a canticle—is occasionally included. We learn how to catch the breath of the Spirit as he moves among the group, prompting first one and then another to offer praise, intercession, confession. Shyly to begin with, but then with increasing confidence, we join in with our own prayers—startling ourselves as God puts thoughts and words into our minds and onto our lips that we know are not of our invention. This direct openness to God and response to his Word is at the heart of charismatic devotion. From obedience to the inspiration of God in little things, such as offering a comment on a scripture passage or saying a few words aloud in prayer, we can move forward to obedience in greater things —interpretation, prophecy, and the ministry of the gifts of healing, of teaching, of leading, and so on.

Many prayer groups have been led to see that one of the purposes of God in the charismatic movement is to raise up a people of praise. A favourite chorus begins:

Praise him in the morning,
Praise him in the noontime,
Praise him when the sun goes down.

Just as the divine office evolved among communities in the Church to offer a continuous chorus of praise to God throughout the day, so charismatic prayer groups see their task as focusing their lives on the Word of God in praise, worship and thanksgiving. The liturgical calendar and the daily lectionary unfolds through the seasons of the year the revelation of God's work of creation and redemption through Jesus Christ. Groups which are able to link their meditations and prayers with official lectionaries acknowledge what it means to be one with the Body of Christ, not only in the local neighbourhood, but throughout the world.

'Rejoice always, pray constantly, give thanks in all circumstances; for this is the will of God in Christ Jesus for you' (1 Thess. 5:16–18). How hard this is for a solo-praying Christian! Yet how gently we are led into a life of constant praise in all circumstances if we are one with a praying group! This is because in a group which is sensitive to the Holy Spirit we experience prayer, not as a series of thoughts and words that originate with us, but as a flow of praise which for ever ascends to the Father through the Son. We relax and settle down to an on-going process 'with angels and archangels and with all the company of heaven.' We let it subtly mould

81

us and sustain us. We do not expect each prayer meeting to take us to the mount of transfiguration, but there are not many meetings when we cannot say in sincerity, 'Master, it is well that we are here' (Luke 9:33).

The prayer group, then, is where we grow more sensitive to the Holy Spirit, learning to register what our normal senses do not register. We have the courage to follow hunches about what God may be saying in a prophecy or to venture into forms of ministry to others that we would never embark on alone. We timidly advance from statements like, 'What does God want me to do?' to, 'The Lord is telling me to do this.' It is also the place where we can learn from our mistakes. Unless we take risks and are willing to seem a fool sometimes, we will never follow the leading of the Spirit.

And we grow in humility as we admit our own needs before our fellow-Christians and receive help from them. We explain what our problem is. Sometimes the strain of bearing it alone comes rushing to the surface of our consciousness and we weep as we tell it. Then we hear the others taking our problem and offering it to God. Words of consolation and a promise of victory emerge through the inspired praying around us. A hand closes over our head and the group becomes a manifestation of the Counsellor to us personally in a mysteriously powerful way. Perhaps a chorus breaks out—the words of a verse shining with a new significance as they speak to us of faith and hope. And in the silence at the end we suddenly realize that our problem has shrunk, if not disappeared. What was needed was a change in us—and God has begun to act.

Eileen was a married woman in her early thirties. She was a regular communicant and attended spasmodically a charismatic house group in the parish. She was not then baptized with the Spirit, but she had been taken to a number of Fountain Trust meetings by one of the members of the group.

One evening during prayer she announced that she was pregnant. When someone began to offer a prayer for her, she burst into tears and said that she had been advised by her doctor to have an abortion. The task of bringing up her two small daughters had been almost too much for her highly-strung personality, and on more than one occasion she had reacted to their naughtiness by acts of cruelty. Her husband, Dick, a man with little religion (I had once invited him to confirmation classes but after several weeks advised him that I could not present him to the bishop because I felt he had no real faith in Jesus Christ), supported his wife in whatever decision she took following the doctor's advice.

During the following two weekly meetings the group showed great sensitivity and concern towards Eileen. It talked through with her the moral arguments for and against the abortion and prayed with her for enlightenment. Finally, she decided against having an abortion on the understanding that the group would continue to pray for her throughout her pregnancy. Within a few weeks she was baptized with the Spirit and a change slowly came over her. Her faith in God matured, she was more content, and her relationships with her two small daughters improved. Her prayers were full of thankfulness and acceptance.

Eventually, after a short, easy labour, a baby boy was born. Within an hour or two I was in the home praying with the happy parents, and the father, holding his new son in his arms, asked me if he could resume his confirmation preparation because he now had a firm faith in Jesus Christ as Lord and Saviour. Salvation meant something very real to him; a son had been saved! Shortly after his confirmation, he was also baptized with the Spirit. When, about a year later, Dick and Eileen moved to another city, their new home became the meeting-place for another charismatic prayer group.

I had a letter from Eileen recently. She wrote:

'Our news, first and foremost—hold on to your hat!—Dick is a Sunday School teacher! It's so unexpected. He suddenly said one morning that he's been reading in a book that fathers should play a greater role in religion, so he thought he'd start teaching the kids at church. After he had gone to work, a friend rang up to say that she had suggested Dick's name as a possible Sunday School teacher to the parish priest. How about that?

'Our house group thrives, and we had two new couples last time. As a result, others are asking about it and want to join. I've been on the telephone just now to a lady who owns a fish and chip shop. She wants to come. Hope she brings some fish and chips with her!

'What a time we've been having, watching the Lord changing people! Two weeks ago a friend of mine came out of church after the eight o'clock service and asked me desperately for a smoke (she'd forgotten to bring her cigarettes with her). I immediately felt myself moved by the Spirit to say, "You don't need a smoke. We'll go back into church and pray."

'What had I said? I wondered. I felt awful as we went back inside. But we prayed, and I spoke in tongues and knew it was of the Lord. Anyway, I've had 'phone call after 'phone call from her since then, telling me how tremendous it is that she's kicked the habit! We have short prayers on the 'phone. Isn't that wonderful?'

(iii)

One group is liable to be very different from another. Like individuals, groups vary enormously. A healthy, well-balanced group, relatively free from inhibitions, goes this way and that, as free as a feather blown by the wind, as the Holy Spirit guides it. It embraces all the vagaries of human nature—cares and hopes, joys and disappointments, shyness and exhibitionism. Sometimes groups get stuck. There is plenty that can go wrong with groups—stories of the damage they can do in a local congregation are legion—but there is a lot more that can go right; and in the forward surge of the renewal movement it is worthwhile taking lots of risks. Provided a group centres its life on the worship of God, then it can be entrusted to his care.

Indeed, worship is central—transformed by being liberated from the restrictions associated with a church building. 'When you come together, each one has a hymn, a lesson, a revelation, a tongue, or an interpretation. Let all things be done for edification' (1 Cor. 14: 26). I used to understand that text simply in terms of participation by the congregation in the formal liturgy, but charismatic prayer groups have given me a new concept of worship as that which the Spirit supplies for the glorification of Christ by his Church. I have taken part in many acts of worship in which there was no rite in the normal sense of that word but in which the 'rite' was inspired within the group as our worship progressed. And it has not been a spontaneous mixture, a haphazard throwing-together of choruses, prayers and scripture-readings. The Spirit bestows his own order on God's people at prayer when we are corporately sensitive to him. Even the eucharistic rite itself can be 'given' in the context of a praying group without using any book but a Bible.

The implications of this are that the difference between formal and spontaneous worship is not as great as we might imagine. Traditional liturgies develop in the Church under the Spirit's guidance, we know, but we do not always appreciate that the Spirit can provide a liturgy by inspiration in and through the group that is open to him. In the nature of things, formal liturgies are more suitable for larger gatherings of Christians; informal liturgies most easily evolve in the smaller group that is accustomed to meeting together for prayer. But both are the gift of the one and the same Spirit who divides to all as he wills.

From worship the group is led out to other kinds of service. Groups tend to specialize in their ministry and mission. One group will concern itself with bringing young people to Jesus Christ, another will tackle the problem of the lonely aged in a neighbourhood, another will engage in ecumenical bridge-building, and so on. But every group walking in the Spirit will witness changes in the lives of its members and in the lives of those with whom it comes in contact. This is the observable sign that the redeeming work of Christ is being continued in the world through the Church.

We cannot measure the love of God in quantitative terms, yet it is a fact of experience that the loving relationship of a small group of Christians has a magnetism and a dynamic that is far, far greater than the sum total of that love which they manifest as individuals. Where two or three are gathered together in Christ's name, he is present with a power that is higher than the simple multiplication of two or three.

Talk of 'cliques' and 'holy huddles' are irrelevant. The group that is solely concerned with itself is already dead to the love of God. But the group that comes together to glorify Christ and to build up his Body is enabled to reach out to others with all the spiritual resources with which God equips those whom he sends in his name. Its members are like the drops of water that create a fountain. They are drawn together and leap towards God as one jet; then, in the sunlight, they sparkle with reflected glory and splash back among their neighbours bringing that glory with them, until it is time for them to be sucked together again for another leap towards God.

Because the Spirit is God's gift to us, it follows that the community which the Spirit creates is God's gift, too. A prayer meeting is not necessarily a collection of close friends. It is the drawing together of those whom God chooses. It has often struck me, in the groups and communities to which I have belonged, that while God uses friendships in their formation, he also transcends such friendships and brings together individuals who might not be close to one another in more casual circumstances. This is why care has to be taken in the formation of prayer meetings in a parish, by the clergy or by those who initiate them. We should pray about the increase in the size of the fellowship and test each suggestion of a new member by seeking God's will. No new-comer should be introduced without first consulting the rest of the group. The majority of members must be sympathetic towards a charismatic style of Christian devotion otherwise the group will be hindered in its praying and ministry. There will be suspicions occasionally among those in the congregation who are not in a group that these prayer meetings are for a select few. The advantage of having a larger assembly in a parish is that enquirers can be taken along to it to learn more of the charismatic movement before being introduced to a house group.

(iv)

A common feature of meetings and groups is that, if they are led by the Spirit, God endows one or more of their members with the charism of leadership. 'Having gifts that differ according to the grace given to us, let us use them . . ., he who gives aid, with zeal' (Rom. 12: 6, 8). 'Gives aid' does not convey all that is meant by *proistēmi*. Its basic sense is that of 'standing before' and so comes to mean 'take a lead.' This is how the N.E.B. translates the phrase, 'If you are a leader, exert yourself to lead.' In 1 Corinthians 12: 28 Paul uses another word, *kybernēsis*, 'administrators' in the R.S.V. but 'power to guide (others)' in the N.E.B. The word is the source of our modern 'cybernetics,' the scientific study for the control of systems which formed the basis for the development of computers. Originating in Greek as a technical term for 'steering' a ship, it implies a leadership which is able to guide others into fulfilling the will of God for them and for the community. This is the gift we should expect to be given within a group.

The leaders are the immediate pastors of its members. They organize the meetings, arrange the programme, encourage participation by all, and care for individuals. In parishes and local congregations where house groups meet, it is usual for the leaders to gather regularly with the priest or minister for prayer and consultation. This gives an opportunity to support a leader who is experiencing difficulties with his group and to supply training in leadership techniques when necessary. The happiest meetings I ever had in a parish were those I shared with the five house group leaders. For me it was an initiation into the strengths provided by God in a team ministry, contrasting sharply with my official position as vicar, a sole minister.

Leaders' consultations are vital for one of the most important and yet most delicate of the leadership roles—the estab-

87

lishment and maintenance of relationships with other groups, and especially with the larger congregation or congregations from which a group's members are drawn. If a prayer meeting is ecumenical, this task can be complicated. It is in an attitude of co-responsibility for other Christian groups and congregations that the prayer meeting is often tested most severely. Divisiveness is such a temptation for those who are conscious that once they were blessed by the Spirit of God and who are anxious to be blessed again! Here more than anywhere they have to depend on the grace of God that his gift of love to them will strengthen the Body of Christ and their place in it. The words of the apostle become especially significant:

'Love is patient and kind; love is not jealous or boastful; it is not arrogant or rude. Love does not insist on its own way; it is not irritable or resentful; it does not rejoice at wrong, but rejoices in the right. Love bears all things, believes all things, hopes all things, endures all things. Love never ends' (1 Cor. 13:4–8).

'Thus each group of Christians will learn its utter dependence upon the whole Body. It will indeed be aware of its own immediate union with Christ, but it will see this experience as a part of the one life of the one family in every age and place. By its dependence upon the Church of history it will die to self-consciousness and self-satisfaction. And as with the group, so with the individual Christian; he will know his dependence upon the other members of the Body, wherein the relation of member to member and of function to function begets humility and love. The gifts that he possesses belong to the Body, and are useful only in the Body's common life. Thus through membership he dies to self-sufficing, and knows that his life in Christ exists only as a life in which all the members share.'[3]

NOTES

[1] John Poulton, *A Today Sort of Evangelism*, Lutterworth Press, 1972, p. 89.
[2] John Taylor, *The Go-Between God*, S.C.M. Press, 1972, p. 126.
[3] A. M. Ramsey, *The Gospel and the Catholic Church*, Longmans, 1936, p. 44.

CHAPTER IX

HIS OWN FAMILY

(i)

'I'VE got a new wife!' cried a middle-aged husband joyfully to us as he came down the main staircase at Whatcombe, his arm round his smiling partner.

'And I've found a new husband!' she declared, hugging him in a way one rarely sees a wife of her age hugging her spouse in public.

They had every reason to rejoice. A few weeks' previously their marriage had been almost dead. Then there had been counselling, repentance, the awakening of a desire to receive all that God offered them, and baptism with the Holy Spirit. They were happy, they looked younger, they praised the Lord.

Married couples who are baptized with the Spirit frequently enter into deeper relationships with one another, mentally, psychologically and physically. I have seen marriages at breaking-point renovated in love, and couples entering into a second and more wonderful honeymoon through God's grace. The reason is, perhaps, not difficult to explain. At the time of their courtship many Christians do not pray together and test their relationship before God. Do we have the charism of marriage? is not a question that is asked among the wedding preparations! If someone thinks he has a gift of healing, it is relatively easy to test this. He simply prays with a sick person and lays hands on him. But if two people think that they have the charism of marriage, this will only be confirmed when, after seeking God's will, they marry.

The situation illustrates the fact that we do not have the absolute certainty about any of the gifts of the Spirit. To expect that we shall always exercise a particular charism is to overlook the fact that we rely constantly upon God for spiritual gifts. He requires us to take risks believing that he will fulfil his promises.

The first question a man or woman should ask is not, Who is the right person for me? but, For whom am I the right partner? A truly Christian marriage looks first at the will of God and then at the needs of the partner. But then it looks further, for marriage is the spiritual gift of life fellowship which is capable of supporting two people and going beyond them to others. Charisms, we repeat, are 'for the common good.' God leads two people together to make one another happy so that others, too, can be made happy through them. A Christian marriage reaches out from the community of the husband, wife and children to the congregation and the society within which God has put them. Husband and wife from a miniature Church—the smallest possible fellowship of the Holy Spirit—for ministry and mission in the name of Christ to those around them.

Larry Christenson's *The Christian Family* (Fountain Trust, 1971) has been influential in charismatic circles in Britain and America. Based on a book by H. W. J. Thiersch published in Germany over a hundred years ago, it expounds the principles of Christian family living from the New Testament in an uncompromising way. The author asserts that there is a firm, unalterable decree of God about the position of men and women in marriage, established by their creation and found in the nature of both, and this decree is filled with grace by the Gospel, not overturned by it.

A key text is 1 Corinthians 11: 3, 'The head of every man is Christ, the head of a woman is her husband, and the head of Christ is God.' If we consider the meaning of this headship in the light of the Creeds, says Christenson, we know that submission cannot mean inferiority, or we would be saying that Christ is inferior to the Father—and the Church battled for centuries to establish that he is coequal with the Father. Christ is, therefore, both submissive to the headship of the Father and coequal with him. This, continues the author, is the pattern of relationships within marriage. Although she is

90

submissive to her husband, the wife is not inferior; indeed, by the divine analogy, she is coequal. The relationship is a functional one, just as the relationship between the Father and the Son in the mystery of the Trinity is a functional one. 'The Father delights to exalt the Son and the Son exalts the Father. The husband should likewise exalt his wife and seek in every way to honour her. The wife will find the same joy in submitting to her husband as Christ does in submitting to the Father.'[1]

In practical terms this means that the husband takes the ultimate responsibility for the welfare and discipline of the family while the wife acts within the protective support of her husband. After many years of marriage counselling, Christenson contends that most of the unhappiness and failures in families can be traced to the failure of the partners to function within these roles. Furthermore, he argues, these functions can only be fulfilled if both the husband and the wife recognize that God bestows a spiritual gift on them for this purpose when they are joined together as man and wife in his name. Commitment to one another in the little community of marriage, like the commitment of Christians to one another in the community of the Church, enables the Lord to pour his grace upon them for his glory and for their edification.

Christenson sees parents exercising a special kind of priesthood on behalf of their children. The vocation of a priest, he points out, is to represent God to the people, and to represent the people to God. In Christ all Christians exercise this priesthood in the Church; but in the family parents exercise it in a special way. First, they present God to their children. This they do through example, through teaching, through leading in various forms of family worship. Second, they present their children to God. This they do through family prayer and through introducing their children to the life and liturgy of the Church. With the grace of God, this priestly ministry of parents brings their children to a real experience of the heavenly Father's love and awakes in them a desire to worship and serve Jesus Christ. Religious difficulties in later

91

life often stem from the fact that parents never exercised this ministry properly. A man who has known only an unloving father has to be healed to the depths of his psyche before he can begin to understand what it means to have a loving Father as God.

Shortly after the book was published, the author was sitting in the auditorium at a conference when a man came up to him and said, 'The first time I read that book I wanted to burn it. The second time I thought it might have an idea or two. The third time I said, "Praise the Lord!" '

This has been the reaction of many readers (I have used it in house groups as a book to study and observed young husbands and wives swing round in their opinions about it). Yet it has helped many Christian marriages over difficulties. Its scriptural foundation is difficult to fault, and its value as a home-mender is incalculable. The teaching is basically charismatic: when God calls his people to undertake a task for him, he calls them in community, changes them, and equips them through that community with his grace for the task.

The same is true of those who are called by God to the celibate life. Paul regarded celibacy, like marriage, as a charism: 'I wish that all were as I myself am. But each has his own special gift from God, one of one kind, and one of another' (1 Cor. 7:7). Some people remain unmarried because they are afraid of responsibility for another person, or because they are too concerned for themselves. This is not the gift of celibacy. Celibacy is a charism for those whom Jesus summons to be eunuchs for the sake of the kingdom of God. Like marriage, the gift can make a person happy only if he is willing, through the advantages of his single state, to be responsible for others. True celibacy is to be unattached to one person in order to be available for all. Roman Catholic priests affirm that, after being touched by the Holy Spirit, their celibate lives took on a new meaning; they saw themselves as the recipients of a precious gift from God for being effective instruments in the name of Jesus Christ. It is tragic that the modern Western world, with its fears about heterosexual and homosexual relationships, makes it so difficult for Christian people to approach the matters of marriage and celibacy from a truly scriptural viewpoint.

(ii)

One way in which the Holy Spirit is equipping both the married and the unmarried today is in giving the charisms of fellowship to gather them into communities who live, pray and work together for his glory in the Church. This is another striking feature of the contemporary religious scene—and especially of the charismatic movement.

The impulse towards a common life is, of course, as old as the Christian Church. One of the results of the gift of the Spirit was the foundation of the Jerusalem community: 'And all who believed were together and had all things in common; and they sold their possessions and goods and distributed them to all, as any had need. And day by day, attending the temple together and breaking bread in their homes, they partook of food with glad and generous hearts' (Acts 2: 44-46). These verses have been the inspiration of thousands of different forms of Christian community throughout the centuries. Living together in the name of Jesus Christ, they have ordered their shared life so that the worship of God leads into the service of others. In the history of the religious orders we receive much of the history of Christendom.

The present movement is towards forms of community within urban situations as well as in large houses. One of the best-known examples of an urban Christian community is that established among the members of the Episcopal Church of the Redeemer in Houston, Texas, where a proportion of the congregation live in small households—single people of the same sex living together in houses, other single people sharing in the home of one or more married couples and their children. At the time of writing there are over forty of these households. Arrangements are made whereby some members go to work and others remain at home to deal with domestic matters. All the households engage in ministry in the Church

93

and in the neighbourhood. 'The Fishermen, Inc.', was set up by the rector, Father Graham Pulkingham, to give new ministries a flexible administrative structure while keeping them within the life of the parish. Among the ministries included are the running of a coffee-house as a meeting-point with others (the *Way Inn* keeps in touch with about a thousand young people), a legal advice bureau for those in Houston who cannot afford the services of a lawyer, a medical clinic, a bookshop and a publications department. Interest in the Houston community has been shown all over the world and 'The Fisherman, Inc.' is now engaged in ministries in different countries. At the invitation of the bishop, a Houston-type community was begun in a suburb of Coventry called Potter's Green in 1972, with the intention of seeing if this form of household could be adapted to the English scene.[2]

The Word of God community in Ann Arbor, Michigan, is similar to Houston but stretches across congregations. It began among Roman Catholic staff and students of the University of Michigan, but is now wider in its social representation and has become entirely ecumenical. Ann Arbor engages in a variety of ministries, and it has become the centre of the Catholic Pentecostal movement in north America. Its monthly magazine, *New Covenant*, has a large circulation and fulfils a need similar to that fulfilled by the Fountain Trust's magazine, *Renewal*, in this country.

Another model is in the congregation of the Anglican cathedral in Sidney, Australia. A community has grown up within the parish, which is in a downtown part of the city. The oversight of the community is shared both by community members and by members of the parish who are not in the community. In this way the community avoids being separate from the parish but is built into its life and structure. The community has one of the clergy as its chaplain.

In England developments of this kind have been on a smaller scale. Portal House in Romford, Essex, sprang out of a conviction that God was calling a group of Christians to minister to people in need in the context of an extended family. This is producing similar households in Essex. Infor-

94

mation about new communities and plans for communities comes round at frequent intervals from Sheffield, from Lytchett Minster near Poole, from Crawley, from Birmingham—the list is steadily growing. It is likely to become a widespread feature of local church life in the future.

The Barnabas Fellowship at Whatcombe House is an example of a community living as one household in a single building. The founder members were two married couples, Reg and Lucia East with their three children, and Ron and Jean Dodgson with a grown-up son. In the two years since its foundation in 1971 it has remained about nine members—another married couple with a son and three single people. Our chief work is the organising of conferences, mostly for groups from parishes, clergy, and members of other communities, to assist in building up stronger fellowships in parishes and other groups through the insights and experiences of the charismatic movement. By living in community ourselves, we find we are able to contribute something from our own experience of the strengths and difficulties of living closely as one.

(iii)

After two years we are beginning to learn some of the essentials of community living in the Spirit.

First, we must be committed to a discipline of daily prayer together. We have not adopted the traditional pattern of saying offices. Instead, we spend time in meditative Bible study, waiting on God, and free prayer each day. Offices are used on other occasions. The daily face-to-face confrontation round the Word of God followed by prayer forces us to look at relationships between ourselves, between ourselves and God, and between ourselves and the work which we undertake with others in his name.

Secondly, we must be willing to let God change us as persons. The process of gradual transfiguration which the Holy Spirit works through ordinary congregational life, and especially through the prayer groups described in the last

95

chapter, is sharpened and deepened when people live together. Indeed, we sometimes feel that we are in a laboratory as specimens in divine experiments! But, through the discussions and prayers together over weeks and months, we see little miracles take place in one another. The meditations of Jeremiah in the potter's workshop often come into our minds:

'I went down to the potter's house, and there he was working at his wheel. And the vessel he was making of clay was spoiled in the potter's hand, and he reworked it into another vessel, as it seemed good to the potter to do. Then the word of the Lord came to me: "O house of Israel, can I not do with you as this potter has done? says the Lord. Behold, like the clay in the potter's hand, so are you in my hand" ' (Jer. 18:3–6).

Thirdly, we must be committed to one another, in time and abilities as well as in the sharing of possessions and money. It is only by being committed to one another that God is able to take our abilities, crown them in a natural and sometimes supernatural way with the grace of his spiritual gifts, and use each one of us for the ministry of the whole community to the Church. Looking back, it is remarkable how he has drawn together at Whatcombe people of very different backgrounds and professions, and how he uses each one of us differently— lecturing, counselling, leading worship, office work, catering, decoration, gardening, and so on. At one time we used to think that every member of the community should have a hand in every job. Now we are beginning to realize that God's way is to use people according to different abilities and charisms. But even with our special tasks, we try to do everything as for one another. For example, the fact that I am sitting at my desk writing this book at the moment is because the other members of the community believed that it is God's will that I should do so. I did not undertake the commission to produce it without consulting them first.

Fourthly, we must accept one another totally in spite of different Christian traditions. We represent wide varieties of churchmanship, from Free Evangelical and Anglican Evangelical to Anglo-Catholic, and we have to seek the Spirit's leading through various difficulties caused by this. But the experience is enormously enriching, and I have learned much about ecumenicism as a movement of acceptance and love among differing Christians rather than as a means of producing acceptable schemes for institutional Churches (and I write as a former diocesan ecumenical officer!). In the end, reunion is God's gift because it is a manifestation of the love which he gives his people through the Holy Spirit. And it has evangelistic fruits, as the popular chorus sings:

We are one in the Spirit we are one in the Lord;
We are one in the Spirit, we are one in the Lord.
And we pray that all unity may one day be restored,
And they'll know we are Christians by our love, by our love,
Yes, they'll know we are Christians by our love.

But community living is costly. Those who dream of community as a glorious solution to their personal problems find the reality slapping them with a sharp, cold shock! Daily living, praying and working together highlights weaknesses within oneself with frightening clarity!

The married couples in the community have to surrender much of their family privacy to include into their concern the needs of other couples, other couples' children, and other single people. The unmarried have to learn to live for the married and their children, not just for themselves. The children, too, have to adjust to having more adults in the home than is customary in our age.

Living in community does not mean that my personality (or anyone else's) has to be suppressed—though there are certain aspects of my individuality which have to die. Rather, it is an opportunity for the maturing of my personality in growing union with the personalities of others, as all are taken, broken, melted and moulded in the hands of the Potter.

On a day when we as a community are facing up to a test in our relationships and feeling disjointed, it is not unusual for a guest at Whatcombe to remark on the atmosphere of peace and unity they feel among the members of the Barnabas

97

G

Fellowship. At one time I used to be amazed when I heard such remarks. How could that person be so insensitive not to recognize the strain we were under? I used to ask myself. Now I am no longer amazed. I know that the atmosphere of peace and unity which guests experience is not of our making but is brought into being through what God is creating out of our commitment to one another. It doesn't matter if you disagree; it only matters if you cease to be a channel of God's love. 'Beloved, let us love one another; for love is of God, and he who loves is born of God and knows God' (1 Jn. 4:7).

The strength which God supplies to the individual through the community is tremendous. It seems that it is when we are most weak in ourselves that we are most powerful in God. 'My grace is sufficient for you, for my power is made perfect in weakness' (2 Cor. 12:9). I know that when I am away from the community, engaged in a ministry of public speaking on their behalf, I am vividly aware of their presence and support when I stand before an audience. 'I am with you in spirit' is not an empty phrase; it proclaims a reality experienced by those who, though separated geographically, are one in the Spirit. Power in togetherness—that is why Christian theology has always insisted that the Spirit is manifested to and through the individual inasmuch as he is united to the Church.

In an essay on the emergence of Christian communities in the U.S.A. in the wake of Roman Catholic Pentecostalism Bertil W. Ghezzi writes:

'We have come to understand that this formation of Spirit-led communities was no accident. Wherever the Lord pours out his Holy Spirit, he draws men together in unity. This is true now as it was in apostolic times. As we grow in our understanding of what the charismatic renewal is and where it is going, he continues to deepen our knowledge of the connection between being filled with the Holy Spirit and living as one in the Body of Christ. . . . The calling together of a particular people is a fresh new thing the Lord himself is doing. He is re-peopling the face of the earth.'[3]

NOTES

[1] *New Covenant,* Volume 2, Number 11, May 1973, p. 1.
[2] Described by the rector, Graham Pulkingham, in *Gathered for Power,* Hodder, 1973.
[3] From a contribution entitled, 'Three Charismatic Communities', in *As the Spirit leads Us,* edited by Kevin and Dorothy Ranaghan, Paulist Press, New York, 1971, p. 186. This book is a sequel to the Ranaghans' *Catholic Pentecostals,* Paulist Press, 1969, which tells how the charismatic movement first influenced Roman Catholics in the U.S.A.

CHAPTER X

ONE BODY, ONE SPIRIT

(i)

'WHERE the Spirit of the Lord is, there is freedom' (2 Cor. 3:17). When the Holy Spirit touches us, we find ourselves being gradually freed from the things that bound us in the past—prejudices and dislikes as well as sinful habits and material concerns. The pentecostal experience is sometimes called 'a release in the Spirit.' This is certainly how it affects people as they realize more fully the invisible and permanent blessings of Jesus Christ and gradually reject the pleasures, possessions and powers of this world. 'Those who live according to the Spirit set their minds on the things of the Spirit' (Rom. 8:5).

But 'freedom' is a much-abused word these days, and it is essential that we should understand what kind of a liberty we are given in the Spirit. It is not the kind that releases us from obligations. That must be obvious from what I have described in this book. Rather, it is a total personal submission to the yoke of Jesus Christ so that we may enter into the total freedom of God himself. 'For freedom Christ has set us free,' Paul told the Galatian congregations; 'stand fast therefore, and do not submit again to the yoke of slavery' (5:1). 'Take my yoke upon you, and learn from me,' Jesus invited his disciples; 'for I am gentle and lowly in heart, and you will find rest for your souls. For my yoke is easy, and my burden light' (Mt. 11:29–30). The freedom of the Spirit, then, is freedom in Jesus Christ. It is a freedom *for* Jesus and *for* others, not for ourselves. By entering into the liberty of God's children, we can be used by him for his purposes through his Church.

Through his Church. I have tried to stress this qualification. The Body of Christ is not the charismatic prayer group that we go to on Wednesday evenings any more than it is the congregation at the parish communion on Sunday mornings; it is not the community at Whatcombe House and their guests any more than the people in Salisbury Cathedral thirty miles away. The Body of Christ is all these and all other faithful Christians, living and departed; and it is through them —through all of them—that the Holy Spirit comes to us, seizes hold of us, and uses us to glorify Jesus Christ.

It is too easy for a charismatic prayer group or community to see itself over against the organized Church. Because you have had a certain experience of God's grace, it is tempting to think in terms of 'them' and 'us'—'them' being the unfortunates who have not had that experience! But everything in scripture and Christian history flashes warnings against such an attitude. The Spirit is not limited in the ways he works in people. God pours out his Spirit on all flesh to make us *one*. And as the individual is given the Spirit for the common good as found in his group or congregation, so the prayer group is given the Spirit for the common good as found in their congregation or the deanery, and so on. We are co-responsible for one another within the boundaries that God sets, not those set by our movement or our denomination. The Lord, it seems, often has to tell his people:

'Enlarge the place of your tent, and let the curtains of your habitations be stretched out; hold not back, lengthen your cords and strengthen your stakes. For you will spread abroad to the right and to the left, and your descendants will possess the nations and will people the desolate cities' (Is. 54: 2–3).

Yet those swept into the charismatic movement do feel a tension between themselves as Christians baptized with the Spirit and entering into a new liberty, and themselves as churchmen committed to established institutions which sometimes seem far removed from what they believe the Holy Spirit is doing in them and around them among their friends. So it seems a useful exercise to close this little book with a discussion on the question which Father Emmanuel Sullivan asks at the end of his report on the movement, drawn up for

101

the British Council of Churches: 'How is the pentecostal movement to be related to the renewal of the Christian Church?'[1]

Because pentecostalism is neither a denomination nor a doctrine but a spirituality and a way of living that stems from it, the movement brings new life into any context—Anglican, Baptist, Methodist, Roman Catholic, United Reformed. I did not find that my experience and what followed from it incompatible with my vocation as an Anglican and an ordained priest. Rather, it enabled me to look at my Church and my calling with new eyes and find in them many signs of God's work that I had not noticed before. The forms of the Spirit were around me in the Church of England's ministries, liturgies and institutions.

For those involved in the charismatic movement, then, it is not so much a question of divided loyalties as a yearning to see institutional Churches come alive again with the Spirit who made them what they are and who still dwells within them. The picture of the Spirit as a flowing river is an apt one. He moves among men forging a new path and the river is formed—the institutional Church. Then the water is diverted into other paths, but the outline of the old river remains with a small stream of water in its bed as a reminder of what it once was.

There has to be wisdom in this matter. On the side of the charismatic there needs to be a constant reminder that since the Church was instituted by Jesus Christ, there is a sense in which she will always be institutional. If baptism in water and the Spirit means entering into relationships with large numbers of people, then there must be structures within which those relationships are built up. If hearing the Word of God results in a response from people, then there must be machinery through which that response can express itself in decision-making and plans for action. If the breaking of the bread is a sign of the continuing fellowship among people, then there must be structures for ordering its administration and discipline.

And the charismatic must not be blind to the obvious signs of the Spirit's activity in the institutional Churches now. The stream in the old river bed may not be as abundant and fast-flowing as we would wish, but it is still water and it is still flowing. Although we hear about declining church member-ship and a fall off in the number of ordinations, there are plenty of other things to encourage us.

Much genuine devotion to our Lord and a concern for evangelism are plainly evident. A new craving for religious experience has suddenly sprung up and begun to spread, especially among the young. Churchmen are seeking a per-sonal encounter with God and an authentic faith that moves mountains—though often expressed in a determination that church services should be 'meaningful' and 'relevant.' Retreats, quiet days, and similar spiritual exercises have never been more popular—provided they are planned with inspired imagination. Pilgrimages to holy places—ancient cathedrals, Walsingham, Glastonbury, Iona—are undertaken by thou-sands in official and unofficial parties. Sales of paperbacks on spirituality reach new records. *Jesus is alive!* stickers pro-liferate—and not only for decorative purposes. Christian giving is proportionately higher than ever before. More adults are coming forward for confirmation, and the numbers of men entering the Church of England's auxiliary ministry increases each year.

Alongside these signs are other pointers to the Spirit's work. There is a general unease among clergy and laity that the Churches are not meeting the deeper needs of the human spirit in their teaching and ritual. They are realizing that the slickest expositions of Christian doctrine and the tidiest presentations of contemporary liturgies can be dead without a renewal of faith. Furthermore, they are becoming uncom-fortably conscious that the life-style of many local churches does not proclaim a God who is living and speaking and act-ing through his people here and now. They know only too well that a congregation whose main concern appears to be the raising of funds for a new roof, or the maintenance of an annual routine of one social event after another, will never be accepted as 'a holy temple in the Lord.' If Christianity is going to appeal today, it will do so for one reason only—it must be authentic. And that means that local congregations must be *experienced* as what they claim to be, 'households of faith' and 'dwelling places of God in the Spirit.'

But on the side of the institution—that is, those in the ecclesiastical structures who govern and administer, from the parochial church councils and deanery synods in the Church of England up to the General Synod and the boards in Church House—there needs to be an awareness and an openness to what God is doing among his people. The institutional Church can never be run like a machine which has to be kept grinding through repetitive processes year after year. It must be kept informed and flexible, its officials aware of the charism which gives them their office and praying constantly for guidance to be shown what their role is to be in the ongoing flood of the Spirit. To lead is a spiritual gift, as we have seen, and a true leader in Christ shares in our Lord's prophetic ministry as well as his priestly and royal one.

Church leaders are often frightened by revivalist movements lest they should be engulfed in the extravagances which have characterised some movements in the past, or lest they should be forced into positions where their responsibilities are seriously compromised. But if bishops, clergy and church councils treat pentecostalists in their dioceses and parishes with distant tolerance or hesitant suspicion, they can hardly expect a healthy spiritual growth in the Church as a whole.

In the spring of 1973 Cardinal Suenens visited the Word of God community in Ann Arbor, Michigan. During the course of this, he was asked how he, as a Roman Catholic, saw the charismatic movement in its relation with his Church. He replied: 'If we stop with the structural changes—parish councils, synods of bishops, and so forth—we have merely reached the sociological level, not the spiritual. The people in these structures need to be alive in the Holy Spirit and sensitive to his action if they are truly to promote life, and not merely engage in sterile confrontation and the exchange of human opinions. For example, when we come to the bishops' synods, we bishops need to be more concerned with being open and sensitive to the Holy Spirit than with defending our positions. That is very difficult to do, but without this genuine openness and sensitivity to the Holy Spirit, we won't be able to follow the Lord into the full renewal he really has for the Church.'[2]

Perhaps, then, we should put Father Sullivan's question the other way round. If the charismatic movement is truly of God—and I have yet to encounter any informed criticism that even begins to raise a reasonable doubt in my mind—then we should not ask, How is the pentecostal movement to be related to the renewal of the Christian Church? but, How is the Christian Church to be related to the renewal of the pentecostal movement?

(iii)

The strength of the movement, as we have seen, derives from the fact that the individual's personal experience of baptism with the Holy Spirit leads to the emergence of a group of Christians who are committed to one another and to the whole Church. When this fact is related to the present-day life and practice of the Church of England, certain possibilities begin to offer themselves.

The rites of Christian initiation—baptism, confirmation and first communion—assume that when an individual is made a member of the Church he is plunged into the life and fellowship of the Spirit. The charismatic movement has revealed our weaknesses in appreciating what this means. Charisms such as speaking in tongues give the individual Christian a profound awareness of the reality of the Spirit's presence within him and encourage him to seek further charisms for the common good. In preparing people for initiation—or in preparing them for that part of the initiation rite which remains uncompleted, that is, confirmation and first communion—we should lead them to expect a new in-filling with the Holy Spirit at or about the time that they receive the laying on of hands by the bishop and their first communion. The fact that many of our confirmation candidates are young should not deter us. Young people receive the Holy Spirit easily and naturally if they are taught what to expect—and the results are just as remarkable as when older people are involved.

Our assessment of the right moment for a person's confirmation will be governed by our discernment of what God is doing in him or her. When an individual begins to exercise his charisms for building up the local church, and when the fruits of the Spirit begin to appear in his dealings with his neighbours, that is the time for him to be presented to the bishop for the laying on of hands. The old collect used at a confirmation service asks God not only to strengthen the candidate but also to increase in him the manifold gifts he has already received. The prayer rightly acknowledges that standing before the bishop is a person who has not only been brought to Christ by repentance and faith, but is also one in whom the Spirit is already working for the redemption of the world.

For the newly baptized and confirmed, as for most members of the congregation, the local church must manifest her charismatic nature. Unless there is a fellowship of the Spirit to be confirmed into, confirmation makes little sense. While regular meetings of Christians in large numbers for worship in churches will always be necessary—at least, in the foreseeable future—there is little doubt that the small group fulfils individuals' needs for fellowship more satisfactorily and provides better opportunities for Christians to minister.

This must be obvious by now. The group is no newcomer to the English ecclesiastical scene. Throughout the 'sixties various campaigns and schemes, culminating in the *People Next Door* project sponsored by the British Council of Churches, brought together Christians of different denominations in groups of about a dozen or so, and these gave an impetus to the establishment of the house meeting as the place where they encountered one another face-to-face. Adult education in the Churches has shifted into the behavioural sciences and introduced clergy and laity to methods of sensitivity training to equip them for leadership and maintenance tasks within the small group situation. What the charismatic movement is doing is taking the small group and showing how it can rely on the resources which God the Holy Spirit provides for its ministry in the Church.

If the Church of England freed its clergy and its people so that their lives could be based on Spirit-filled groups which met human needs with the authority of Jesus Christ, there would be little point in evangelistic campaigns and calls to mission. The Gospel would be proclaimed through lives seen to be changing, through healings witnessed, through the love of God experienced within Christian groupings and communities.

In effect, the world is saying to the Church today, 'If Jesus is alive, *show* us.' And in view of what the Church stands for, this is not an unreasonable request. It might be argued in reply that Jesus told the Pharisees, 'The kingdom of God is not coming with signs to be observed' (Lk. 17:20). But that is not a correct use of the text, for the world's request is not pharisaical. It is a genuine request to see Jesus. The text we should turn to is in Christ's exhortation, 'You are the light of the world. A city set on a hill cannot be hid. Nor do men light a lamp and put it under a bushel, but on a stand, and it gives light to all in the house. Let your light so shine before men, that they may see your good works and give glory to your Father who is in heaven' (Mt. 5:14–16).

What impressed people in the apostolic age was not only the preaching but the 'many wonders and signs done through the apostles' as well as the fellowship of the Christians (Acts 2:43). The Church prayed, 'Lord, grant to thy servants to speak thy word with all boldness, while thou stretchest out thy hand to heal, and signs and wonders are performed through the name of thy holy servant, Jesus' (Acts 4:29–30). And we are told that the place in which they were gathered was shaken and they were all filled with the Holy Spirit and spoke the Word of God with boldness. That is a mark of the apostolic age which we in the Church of England (and in the other Churches) urgently need to be given today.

I have already pointed out that the charismatic leader of the house group is a key figure in establishing and maintaining the relationships between his group and the local congregation. We might say that this relationship illustrates the question we have posed: the leader represents the movement; the parish priest, as head of the local congregation, represents the institution. But charism and office cannot be so divided. If the institutional Church is to integrate with pentecostalism, represented by the house group leader, then she must recognize that, after a suitable period of testing, the gift of God to that individual should be sealed by his ordination to the order of priesthood. This becomes a matter of some importance when the house group develops as a 'little church' and begins to celebrate the eucharist.

The Church of England still expects candidates for the auxiliary ministry to qualify for the General Ordination or its equivalent. If a man is to replace (on a part-time basis) the parish priest, this is understandable; but the leader of a house group is being called to minister at a different level, and to remove him from the group among whom and for whom the charism of leadership has been given by the Holy Spirit in order to give him academic training, is to remove him from the very environment in which the most valuable training will be received.

Finally, when we turn to that most characteristic of Church of England institutions, the Sunday morning service, we can learn something from charismatic assemblies.

Our worship needs to be humanized and Spirit-filled—in that order! Whether it is a parish communion or morning prayer, participants must be helped to feel that they are taking part in a *human* activity. It is a principle of worship that we approach God as created beings in need of his grace. Rite and ceremony have their great, traditional value in helping us to make this approach; but where traditional rites or ceremonies leave us with the impression that we are being treated as less than human—or as humans of an earlier century—then reform is necessary. In assembling for worship, our congregations should feel that it is a normal, human activity that they are about to participate in.

Then we should lead them to participate as those who are being filled by the Spirit to glorify Jesus Christ. This does not mean disorder! The priest who presides at the service controls the proceedings, but he does this with a relaxed authority, showing that he understands the spiritual gift he is called to exercise in the congregation—namely, the charism of leadership to assist the people of God as they offer praise and thanksgiving to their living Lord in the Spirit. There is a place for reverence and silence in worship, as there is for confession and petition. But there is also a place for joy—the joy that springs up from men and women whose hearts God has touched. It is this joy that is often absent in our parish churches and cathedrals. From classical Pentecostalism we can learn what it means to *celebrate*.

I am not suggesting that our services should be conducted like a West Indian Pentecostalist gathering. I am simply saying that we ought to express our joy in the Spirit in what for us is a normal, human manner when we worship. For we have so much to rejoice about—what God has done in the past, what he is doing now, what he will do in the future.

The Lord is here. His Spirit is with us.

Christ has died:
Christ is risen:
Christ will come again.

Blessing and honour and glory and power be yours for ever and ever. Amen.

Series Three goes some way towards the forms we require (it has a 'full Gospel' flavour that is truly pentecostal!). But when lives are being changed by God, when personal victories are being won in the power of the cross of Christ, and when calls to ministry and mission are being answered in faith by

Christians—then our worship will be Spirit-filled, whatever the rite.

In all that I have described and suggested in this book, especially in the last few pages, dangers abound. I am under no illusions about these—indeed, I have seen some of the dangers myself.

But, then, as Christians we are called to live dangerously. The analogies most frequently used to portray Christian discipleship in the New Testament indicate that following Christ means being prepared to take life-or-death risks. One analogy is making a pilgrimage ('We go up to Jerusalem')—a hazardous undertaking, as the man who fell among thieves discovered. The other analogy is engaging in war ('Fight the good fight of faith').

Yet when we consider our chances in taking risks for Christ—like the man who built a house or the king who went out to war, in the Gospel parables—we know that the resources available to us and to the whole Body of Christ are enormous. 'If God is for us, who is against us? . . . In all these things we are more than conquerors through him who loved us' (Rom. 8:31, 37).

For they are the resources of Christ himself, bestowed on us through the gift of the Holy Spirit. The paschal death and resurrection of Jesus Christ was followed by his glorious ascension to the Father and the pentecostal outpouring of the Holy Spirit; and as a result every Christian becomes 'another Christ' in whom the power of God is manifested. 'Truly, truly, I say to you, he who believes in me will also do the works that I do; and greater works than these will he do, because I go to the Father' (Jn. 14:12).

We have but to claim this promise for ourselves, each one of us.

(iv)

As the Church was being led to a fuller understanding of the nature of God and of the work of the Holy Spirit, Basil, Bishop of Caesarea (d. 379), wrote *De Spiritu Sancto*, a treatise which played an important part in the formation of the doctrine of the Trinity. In it there is a paragraph on the Spirit as the light of God in the Christian which is typical of the theology of Eastern Christendom. It sums up everything that pentecostalism teaches us, and it also says a good deal more:

'When the sun's ray falls on bright and transparent objects, they themselves become radiant and from themselves shed a further shining beam: so the souls inhabited by the Spirit, and illuminated by the Spirit, themselves are rendered wholly spiritual and send out their grace to others. From this source come foreknowledge of the future, the understanding of mysteries, the apprehension of things hidden, the partaking of spiritual gifts, the heavenly citizenship, a place in the choir of angels, unending joy, the power to abide in God, to become like God, and, highest of all ends to which we can aspire, to become divine.'[3]

NOTES

[1] Emmanuel Sullivan, S.A., *Can the Pentecostal Movement renew the Churches?* British Council of Churches, 1972, p. 14.
[2] *New Covenant*, Volume 2, Number 12, June 1973, p. 3.
[3] *De Spiritu Sancto*, 9.23, translated in Henry Bettenson, *The Later Christian Fathers*, Oxford, 1970, pp. 71-72.